What You *MUST* Know About Social Security & Medicare

ERIC R. KINGSON

Introduction by Rep. Edward R. Roybal
Chairman, House Select Committee on Aging

PHAROS BOOKS
A SCRIPPS HOWARD COMPANY
NEW YORK

DEDICATION

To the memory of my Mother, Ethel Schachtel Kingson (1918-1986), who would have enjoyed giving copies of this book to relatives, friends and anyone she met.

And to two special people in her life and mine—Nora Campbell and Elvie Lorig.

Cover design: Elyse Strongin
Book design: Nancy Eato

Copyright © 1987 by Eric R. Kingson

All rights reserved. No part of this book may be reproduced in any form or by an means without written permission of the publisher.

First published in 1987.

Distributed in the United States by Ballantine Books, a division of Random House, Inc., and in Canada by Random House of Canada, Ltd.

Library of Congress Catalog Card Number: 86-062667
Pharos Books ISBN: 0-88687-294-4
Ballantine Books ISBN: 0-345-34397-2

Printed in the United States of America

Pharos Books
A Scripps Howard Company
200 Park Avenue
New York, NY 10166

10 9 8 7 6 5 4 3 2 1

CONTENTS

FOREWORD	4
INTRODUCTION	6
1. THE COMMON STAKE IN SOCIAL SECURITY AND MEDICARE	7
2. SOCIAL SECURITY AND MEDICARE: INSURANCE FOR ALL AMERICANS	13
3. FINANCING SOCIAL SECURITY AND MEDICARE	18
4. SOCIAL SECURITY AND MEDICARE: PAST TO PRESENT	23
5. RECENT CHANGES IN SOCIAL SECURITY	30
6. APPLYING FOR BENEFITS	44
7. DETERMINING YOUR BENEFIT AMOUNT	50
8. RETIREMENT BENEFITS	58
9. SURVIVOR'S BENEFITS	66
10. IF YOU BECOME DISABLED	71
11. MEDICARE BENEFITS	80
12. OTHER PUBLIC PROGRAMS	101
13. THE FUTURE OF SOCIAL SECURITY AND MEDICARE	110
INDEX	119

Foreword

Social Security and Medicare strengthen families and the Nation.

Social Security protects nearly every American, young and old, against the loss of income due to retirement, long-term and total disability, and death. Each month almost 38 million beneficiaries receive Social Security checks. Most are older Americans, including the nearly 27 million retired workers and their spouses, and about 5 million aged survivors of workers, most of whom are widows. Many, however, are not elderly, including the approximately 370,000 surviving spouses caring for young children, the 3 million disabled workers and their spouses, and over 3 million children. Medicare, too, provides partial protection against the cost of hospitalization and medical treatment to about 28 million elderly and 3 million disabled people.

Nothing is free, however. The government collects payroll taxes from approximately 125 million employees (and their employers), and self-employed persons to pay for the Social Security and Medicare programs. In exchange, these workers and their families earn the right to benefits if any of the risks protected against do occur.

Because Social Security and Medicare are essential American institutions, all of us need to know what rights, benefits, and obligations we have under these programs. We also need to understand how they work, so we can assess the problems that will arise from time to time and possible solutions. This book provides such information, including how recent changes in Social Security and Medicare affect you and your family.

This book does not suggest that these programs have been, and will always be, problem free. As you know, early in the 1980's the financing of Social Security was uncertain. Fortunately, in 1983, Congress, with bipartisan support, enacted legislation that ensures the financial solvency of the retirement, survivors' and disability programs for the foreseeable future. (Now, Social Security is actually running substantial yearly surpluses). Similarly, one need only read the newspaper to see that financing problems may arise in the Medicare Hospital Insurance program in the late-1990's, and to learn that Medicare does not adequately protect the elderly and their families from the high cost of long-term care and disabling illnesses. But, we can expect that these and other problems that may arise can be solved in a fair and reasonable way.

ACKNOWLEDGEMENTS

I wish to thank several people and organizations for their generous and helpful assistance. Robert M. Ball, former Commissioner of Social Security; Robert J. Myers, F.S.A., former Chief Actuary of the Social Security Administration and Executive Director of the National Commission on Social Security Reform; and Bruce D. Schobel, F.S.A., Actuary with the Social Security Administration; each reviewed the manuscript, making comments that greatly improved the text. So too did the reviews of Lowell Arye, and Nancy Smith, both on the professional staff of the U.S. House Select Committee on Aging.

Several professionals with the Social Security Administration reviewed the text for factual errors. Richard Getrost, public relations specialist, office of Benificiary Services of the Health Care Financing Administration's Office of Beneficiary Studies and others from that office provided a similar review of the portions concerned with Medicare and Medicaid. The information and public documents provided by offices of the Social Security Administration, and the Health Care Financing Administration, the U.S. House Select Committee on Aging, the U.S. Senate Special Committee on Aging, the American Association of Retired Persons and the National Council of Senior Citizens were very helpful. In acknowledging the assistance of individuals and organizations knowledgeable about Social Security and Medicare, it is important to mention that their review of the manuscript does not imply either agreement or disagreement with the contents, but rather a willingness to share their knowledge.

I also wish to thank The Gerontological Society of America, located in Washington, D.C. and Seven Locks Press of Cabin John, Maryland for permission to utilize material prepared for a report recently released by The Society, *Ties That Bind: The Interdependence of Generations.*

Carolyn Ross of the University of Maryland's School of Social Work and Community Planning provided invaluable secretarial assistance.

Working with Hana Umlauf Lane, Editor-in-Chief of Pharos Books, was a pleasure and made this a better book.

I also wish to thank my wife, Joan Fernbach Kingson, for her patience and support. And I cannot resist mentioning our children, Aaron, age 5, and Johanna, age 2, both of whom I fully expect will be receiving Social Security retirement benefits near the midpoint of the 21st century.

With all this excellent assistance, it should be clear that any errors that may remaining in the text are solely my responsiblity.

Eric R. Kingson
Boston College
Graduate School of Social Work

INTRODUCTION

Although Social Security provides about 40 percent of the income for persons 65 and over, it is far more than a program for the elderly. Benefits are paid to 10 million people under age 65, including over 3 million children. And the economic security that Social Security provides to older persons translates into economic relief for the family members on whom they might otherwise depend.

Despite these benefits, public confidence in the Social Security system has lagged in the past for many reasons. These include the continued talk of financial bankruptcy and recent cuts in benefits. However, according to the 1986 Social Security Trustees Report, the system is adequately financed through the middle of the next century, and recent surveys show that a large majority of young people believe that Social Security is a successful program.

Dr. Eric Kingson's expertise in the area of Social Security is well known. In 1982, Dr. Kingson was a staff member to the National Commission on Social Security Reform. In his current position as an associate professor at Boston College's Graduate School of Social Work, Dr. Kingson has assisted the House Select Committee on Aging on a variety of issues affecting the elderly, including Social Security. His recent testimony before the committee, and a subsequent report by the Gerontological Society of America, demonstrated the importance of intergenerational co-operation in an aging society. Dr. Kingson, the primary author of the report, stressed that Social Security is an excellent program in which all generations have a common stake. And, indeed it is, for Social Security is a family program, one whose protections extend to persons of every age.

As the Chairman of the Select Committee on Aging, I am committed to protecting Social Security and Medicare and other multi-generational programs. The task ahead of us is to continue to restore public confidence in Social Security. Dr. Kingson's book will help to renew public support for this important program, and can serve as a guide for all Americans in understanding the complex workings of Social Security and Medicare.

Chairman Edward R. Roybal
Select Committee on Aging
U.S. House of Representatives

THE COMMON STAKE IN SOCIAL SECURITY AND MEDICARE

Americans of all ages have a common stake in Social Security and Medicare. There are several reasons: Social Security and Medicare benefits are distributed widely across all generations; the programs promote and enhance the dignity and independence of individuals and families; the programs support elderly family members, thereby freeing up the generation in between to direct more resources at their children; Social Security is the heart of the retirement income system, now and for the foreseeable future.

THE VALUE TO BENEFICIARIES

Benefits vary, depending on the recipient's prior earnings, number of eligible family members, and age at initial receipt of benefits. This table shows the average and maximum benefits in January 1987 for different types of beneficiaries.

THE VALUE OF SOCIAL SECURITY IN JANUARY 1987

TYPE OF BENEFICIARY	AVERAGE BENEFIT PER MONTH	MAXIMUM BENEFIT* PER MONTH
Worker Retiring at Age 65*	593*	789*
Retired Worker & Aged Spouse	833	1183*
Surviving Aged Spouse (60+)	444	789*
Disabled Worker	488	1007*
Disabled Worker and Family	890	1570*
Young Surviving Family	1036	1761*

*These figures based on people first reaching age 65, dying, or becoming disabled in January 1987.

Social Security is the primary source of income protection for retirees and their families. Single and married Americans age 65 and over (known for these purposes as the elderly) report that nearly 40 percent of their income comes from Social Security. The remainder comes primarily from other public and private pension benefits (about 14 percent), earnings (about 19 percent), and income from assets (about 22 percent). Plainly, no other source of income is as important to these people, especially those in moderate- and low-income households. In 1984, elderly households with incomes under $10,000 reported that about 70 percent of this money came from Social Security. And 62 percent of all elderly households receiving Social Security said that it provides 50 percent or more of their total income. Social Security is of equally great value to disabled workers, their families, and to the families of deceased workers.

Medicare, too, enhances the well-being of the elderly, the disabled, and people with chronic kidney disease. Not only has it improved access to hospital and physician services for those who are enrolled, but it protects beneficiaries against many of the high and often unexpected costs that accompany illness.

WITHOUT SOCIAL SECURITY

Another way of looking at the value of Social Security is to examine its effect on poverty rates. In 1959, 35 percent of all those aged 65 and over had incomes below the poverty line; in 1985 the figure was 12.6 percent. While the growth of the economy since 1959 has helped remove millions from poverty, improvements in Social Security have been equally important. If Social Security benefits stopped, nearly half of all elderly Americans, more than 13 million people, would have yearly incomes below the poverty line ($6503 for couples and $5156 for singles in 1985), and the size of the welfare rolls would shoot up.

THE STAKE OF YOUNGER WORKERS

Social Security and Medicare are worth a lot to current retirees and their families. The current generation of retirees began collecting benefits relatively early in the life of the program. Like past service credited in a new private pension plan, they did not have to make payroll tax contributions for as many years as future generations of retirees must.

But what do younger workers get for their yearly tax contribution? For one thing, they earn the right to retirement and medical benefits later in life. And many Social Security beneficiaries—nearly 7 million, or about 18 percent—are, in fact, not retired workers, their spouses, or aged widows. Numerous other benefits are earned as well, and these are often overlooked, especially by critics of Social Security.

Social Security and Medicare also protect against loss of income and medical expenses due to disability. And, the survivors insurance program also protects young and middle-aged workers and their families. For example, it is estimated that for a worker age 35 with a non-working spouse age 32 and two children under age six Social Security coverage provides the equivalent of a life insurance policy and a disability insurance policy, each with a face value of about $200,000 in 1985 dollars. And, unlike private pensions, you earn credit toward your Social Security benefits on almost any job you take.

HELPS MAINTAIN LIVING STANDARD

While not intended to replace all earnings lost, Social Security will go a long way toward enabling today's workers and their families to maintain their earlier standard of living at retirement, disability, or death of a breadwinner. The benefit formula guarantees a pension that replaces a relatively constant proportion of pre-retirement earnings—59 percent for the lifetime minimum wage earner, 41 percent for the lifetime average earner, and 28 percent for someone with earnings consistently at the maximum taxable earnings level. In reality, replacement rates are generally lower, mainly because most retirees accept reduced early retirement benefits.

The fact that Social Security is designed to replace a relatively constant proportion of prior earnings for workers at different earnings levels introduces a critical element of stability into the

IMPORTANCE OF VARIOUS SOURCES OF INCOME TO AGED UNITS, 65 AND OVER IN 1984

PERCENTAGE SHARE OF TOTAL INCOME PROVIDED TO

SOURCE OF INCOME	ALL AGED UNITS	UNITS UNDER $5000	$5000-9999	$10,000-19,999	$20,000 or more
Social Security*	39	78	72	49	20
Private Pension	6	1	4	9	6
Public Employee Pension	7	1	3	7	9
Asset Income	28	4	10	21	39
Earnings	16	0	4	10	23
Public Assistance	1	14	3	0	0
Other	2	2	3	2	1

*Includes Railroad Retirement.
Source: Susan Grad, *Income of The Population 55 and Over*, Social Security Administration.

retirement plans of most Americans. For the younger worker, even before receiving benefits, their value is kept up to date with rising wages and the changing standard of living.

Furthermore, the growth in a younger worker's wages will be translated into larger benefits. (Of course, his or her tax contributions will be larger too.) Using reasonable assumptions about the growth of the economy during the next 75 years—about two percent growth per year after inflation—Social Security's actuaries estimate that while a worker earning average wages throughout life and retiring at age 65 in 1986 would receive $576 a month, a similar worker retiring in 2015 would receive $797 a month in 1986 dollars. Of course, the actual dollar amount would be larger. For example, it is estimated that such a worker retiring in 2030 at age 65 will receive a *monthly* benefit of about $5277! But this amount will actually be worth about $918 in 1986 dollars.

Not only does Social Security adjust for changes in the standard of living prior to the receipt of benefits, but, due to increasing life expectancies, future retirees are expected to receive benefits for a longer period of time than today's retirees.

Estimates Of Future Retirement Benefits

YEAR REACHING AGE 65	MONTHLY BENEFIT FOR WORKERS EARNING AVERAGE WAGES* (IN 1986 DOLLARS)	MAXIMUM MONTHLY BENEFITS FOR HIGH-INCOME WORKERS** (IN 1986 DOLLARS)
1986	576	760
2000	689	990
2015	797	1241
2030	918	1434

*for hypothetical worker with average earnings throughout his or her working life and first receiving benefits at age 65.
**for hypothetical worker with maximum taxable earnings throughout his or her life and first receiving benefits at age 65.
Source: Social Security Administration (projected benefits based on Alternative IIB Intermediate Assumptions used in the 1986 Trustees Report).

And younger and middle-aged workers can also count on Social Security to maintain its purchasing power, because the benefits are adjusted automatically for changes in the cost of living. Comparable certainty of inflation protection is simply not available through private pensions or savings.

This is the reason that, while Social Security is not intended to be the only source of income in retirement, it is and will remain the heart of the retirement income system, and of disability and survivors' protection too. It is the building block for the economic well being of retiring, surviving, and disabled individuals and their families, to be supplemented by other pension income, personal savings, and possibly employment.

BENEFITS FOR ALL

But as a recent report issued by The Gerontological Society of America—a national association of scholars, researchers, and practitioners in the field of aging—observes, Social Security and Medicare do more than insure against identifiable risks. They serve other cherished goals and values in our society.

Social Security and Medicare respond to the widespread preference of individuals and families for a non-personal means of support in old age. While much care flows to and from parents and children across their lives, the financial independence of grown children is valued both by them and their parents. Similarly, even in advanced old age, parents do not wish to depend on their children for financial support. Instead, they prefer to rely on a combination of private savings and social insurance programs. Moreover, in the absence of Social Security and Medicare, such responsibilities could overwhelm some families—a possibility that has not escaped the public's notice. (Frequently, what's at risk is leaving families no choice but to have older relatives move in with the family.) And, as noted at the beginning of this chapter, the existence of Social Security and Medicare frees younger and middle-aged family members to invest more resources in their children.

Americans also have a common stake in receiving benefits from Social Security and Medicare as an earned right. Americans generally prefer to avoid means-tested programs. They see welfare programs as demeaning and, as former Secretary of Health, Education and Welfare Wilbur Cohen points out, programs for poor people become poor programs. In contrast, the widespread support for Social Security in this country is partly a result of the fact that workers and their families earn the right to receive benefits through payroll tax contributions.

In short, Social Security and Medicare have value beyond the actual benefits they provide. These programs improve the quality of life for all. By assisting individuals and families in protecting themselves against certain major financial risks, these programs underwrite the dignity of individuals and stabilize family life and the society.

Social Security is one of the finest examples of our society's compassion and wisdom. It holds us together by having us share its costs and benefits. It is costly, but it provides a protection and security to all Americans that money alone cannot buy.

SOCIAL SECURITY & MEDICARE: INSURANCE FOR ALL AMERICANS

Responding to the widespread destitution, unemployment, and social unrest during the Great Depression, Congress passed the Social Security Act in 1935 to insure Americans, through social insurance programs, against large losses of income and to provide public assistance payments for those in financial need. For over 50 years, this act has served as the cornerstone of our social welfare system.

The right to a social insurance benefit, such as Social Security, is established by past earnings in jobs covered by a social insurance program. In contrast, the right to a benefit in public assistance programs, such as Supplemental Security Income (SSI) and Medicaid, is established by financial need.

The original Social Security Act established two social insurance programs—Unemployment Compensation and Old-Age Insurance, then called Old-Age Benefits. The Old-Age Insurance program has evolved into the program we now call Social Security. Medicare was established in 1965. Today, people gen-

---

Social Security in America is one of the truly great achievements of the last fifty years. It contributes greatly to the solution of one of society's most persistent problems—how, when most people depend for their livelihood on earnings, can they be protected against poverty and insecurity when those earnings cease or are greatly reduced.

Robert M. Ball
Former Social Security Commissioner

erally use the term Social Security to include the Old-Age and Survivors Insurance and Disability Insurance programs. Medicare actually includes two programs, Hospital Insurance (HI) and Supplementary Medical Insurance (SMI) for physician's and other medical expenses. The combined cost of Social Security and Medicare for 1987 is approximately $300 billion, nearly 30 percent of the total federal expenditures.

PARALLELS TO PRIVATE INSURANCE?

Social Security and Medicare, like private insurance, make up for losses from identifiable risks. Fundamental to both social and private insurance systems is the ability to identify specific risks and predict the likelihood of these events occurring to individuals participating in the insurance plan. This allows the insurer to set premium rates (payroll tax rates) that cover the costs of the various types of protection in the plan.

Insurance also allows the individual to share his or her risk with other persons in the plan. For example, very few people can afford the cost of replacing a house that burns down. Yet this risk exists for all homeowners. Through the mechanism of insurance, the homeowner pays a relatively small premium, with the insurance company assuming the risk of the financial loss if the house burns down.

Similarly, in exchange for the payroll tax contribution, Social Security and Medicare provide insurance against income loss resulting from risks we all face. For example, without Social Security, many workers disabled at an early age would have to turn to welfare for help. But, because only some of those paying will actually become disabled, a relatively low payment by all provides a monthly benefit for disabled workers and their families that, in most cases, will prevent the extremes of financial hardship.

Like some types of private insurance policies, Social Security helps people save. Brandeis University economist James Schulz points out that without Social Security or other pension plans, the typical worker would have to save about 20 percent of his or her salary per year in order to maintain his or her standard of living after retirement at age 65. With Social Security, saving only about 4 to 7 percent of one's income will do.

But even if you *could* save 20 percent during your working years, there's no guarantee you wouldn't use up your savings by living longer than you'd planned or that you would be sufficiently healthy to work until age 65. And this type of savings is not much help at all in the case of early disability or death.

Like much of private insurance, Social Security and Medicare's Hospital Insurance (HI) program are contributory; this means the right to your benefits is established by your own (or a family member's) work in covered employment and, by implication, by payroll tax contributions. Financing Social Security from payroll taxes also helps ensure its financial responsibility. Benefits promised must be adequately financed.

SOCIAL SECURITY IS COMPULSORY

Unlike private insurance, nearly everyone in the work force must pay Social Security payroll taxes. But, unlike private insurance, no one can be turned down from participating in Social Security, even those who are very sick.

Opponents of Social Security and Medicare's HI program often argue that participation should be voluntary. At first glance, the idea seems appealing, but on closer inspection it becomes obvious that a voluntary program would not work.

If Social Security were voluntary, for example, some people might not save enough to protect themselves and their families. Or they might save enough but invest it foolishly, losing it all. Would the public let them starve, arguing that they should stew in their own juices? Probably not. Most likely, a small public assistance benefit would provide for them. So, one reason Social Security is compulsory is to protect us from the cost of paying for people who might choose not to participate but would later become dependent on public welfare.

A voluntary Social Security or HI program would be left with the most expensive risks. Private insurance companies would most likely accept the healthiest citizens into their plans, leaving the least healthy for the government-run programs. Since no one is turned away from participating in Social Security and Medicare's HI program, participation must be compulsory. This guarantees a fair mix of "good" and "bad" risks.

OTHER DIFFERENCES

Unlike private insurance and private pension plans, Social Security and Medicare are largely pay-as-you-go systems. This means the present generation of workers pay taxes to support current beneficiaries with the understanding that the same will be done for them. This method is often referred to as the social compact between generations.

Early in the life of the program, Congress decided that Social Security should not accumulate full reserves. They are not necessary, anyway. The taxing power of the government stands behind the commitments made by Social Security and Medicare. This guarantees their financial stability. Periodic changes and problems will occur, but neither Congress nor the American people will allow Social Security and Medicare to fail to meet their commitments. That's why these programs do not have to be funded like private insurance and pensions.

There is another important way that Social Security and Medicare differ from private insurance. As Reinhard Hohaus, then an actuary with the Metropolitan Life Insurance Company, wrote in 1938, while private insurance programs are designed to meet the needs of selected individuals for protection against various risks, social insurance meets society's needs to provide a floor of protection for all Americans against critical social hazards. Thus, Social Security and Medicare are designed to provide minimally adequate benefits for nearly all.

HOW MUCH INCOME DOES SOCIAL SECURITY REPLACE?

Retirement experts talk about a three-legged stool of protection with Social Security providing the floor of protection, supplemented by private efforts (private and public employee pension systems, home ownership and other personal savings), and needs-tested programs like Supplemental Security Income (SSI). Social Security is designed to replace some, but not all, earnings lost because of retirement, disability, or death. As noted in Chapter 1, it replaces a higher proportion of previous earnings for low-income workers, but high-income workers receive larger Social Security pensions. Here's why.

Social Security is earnings related. The higher your earnings during your working years, the larger the benefit to which you are entitled. But, it is also concerned with providing adequate benefits for low- and moderate-income workers and families. One way it does this is by providing survivors and family benefits like those for the children of disabled workers. Another way is through the Social Security benefit formula, which gives low-income workers a proportionately larger benefit.

Most highly paid workers are assumed to receive additional income from other pensions and savings. Also, because the higher income worker was in higher tax brackets before retirement, it is not necessary to replace as much of the pre-retirement income as for low earners. Finally, higher income earners receive the lion's share of tax benefits that accompany participation in private pensions and other tax-sheltered savings plans.

It can be argued that for a few workers—some of those with the highest earnings—alternative investments might have a greater rate of return, although such investments involve more risk and do not provide guarantees against inflation. But we should not forget that Social Security offers guarantees and benefits generally unavailable elsewhere, and that without Social Security many would be considerably worse off later in life.

Private pensions, savings, and other investments are desirable and should be encouraged, but none can offer as comprehensive protection to as many as Social Security does.

Financing Social Security and Medicare

There are four Social Security and Medicare trust funds: the Old-Age and Survivors Insurance (OASI) Trust Fund, the Disability Insurance (DI) Trust Fund, the Hospital Insurance (HI) Trust Fund, and the Supplementary Medical Insurance (SMI) Trust Fund. The first three receive most of their income from the payroll taxes you and your employer pay during your working life. For the fourth trust fund, SMI, voluntary premium payments cover about one-quarter of the cost and government contributions from general revenues about three-quarters. Also, the revenues from treating part of Social Security benefits as taxable income go into the OASI and DI Trust Funds and the interest from trust fund investments flows into the Social Security and Medicare funds.

HOW MUCH DO I PAY?

In 1987 workers will make payroll tax contributions on earnings up to $43,800 and employers will match these contributions. Earnings above the taxable earnings base—$43,800 in 1987—are not subject to payroll taxation. The average earner in 1987 will pay about $1320 in payroll-tax contributions, and workers earning at or above the taxable earnings base of $43,800 will pay $3,130.70.

Will payroll tax rates increase? Yes, modest increases are scheduled between now and 1990. The combined OASDHI tax rate (currently 7.15 percent of taxable payroll on employer and employee) is scheduled to rise gradually to 7.65 percent in 1990 and remain at that level thereafter.

Sources For Social Security And Medicare Trust Funds In 1987 (In Billions Of Dollars)*

TRUST FUNDS	FROM PAYROLL TAXES	FROM TAXATION OF BENEFITS	INTEREST ON INVESTMENTS AND OTHER INCOME	PREMIUM PAYMENTS	GOVERNMENT CONTRIBUTION	TOTAL
OASDI	201.3	4.0	4.2	—	—	209.6
I	19.3	0.3	0.6	—	—	20.2
HI	57.8	—	5.0	0.1	—	62.9
SMI	—	—	0.6	7.5	23.2	31.3
Totals	278.4	4.3	10.4	7.6	23.2	324.0

*1986 Trustees Reports, Estimates Based on Intermediate IIB Assumptions.

Also, the 1972 amendments of the Social Security Act provided that the taxable earnings base would be adjusted automatically as average wages increased. For example, the earnings base was increased from $42,000 in 1986 to $43,800 in 1987 to compensate for a 4.3 percent increase in average wages in 1985 over 1984. Without this automatic adjustment, a smaller and smaller proportion of earnings would be subject to payroll taxation as average wages increased.

Once collected, most payroll taxes and other revenues for Social Security and Medicare are paid out in benefits. Additionally, only about 1.1 percent of Social Security revenues are used for administrative expenses, and about 2 percent of Medicare revenues. Funds not needed to pay benefits or administrative costs are invested in U.S. government bonds.

ESTIMATING COSTS

Each year Social Security's and Medicare's Boards of Trustees (the Secretaries of the Treasury, Labor and Health and Human Services, and two public trustees appointed by the President) issue reports on the financial status of the trust funds.

What You Pay For Social Security
(Worker Amount Matched By Employer)

YEAR	% TAX FOR CASH BENEFITS (OASDI)	% TAX FOR MEDICARE (HI)	% TOTAL TAX RATE	TAXABLE EARNINGS BASE	MAXIMUM TAX	TAX ON AVERAGE WAGE EARNER
1983	5.4	1.3	6.7	$35,700	$2,392	$1,016
1984*	5.7	1.3	7.0	37,800	2,646	$1,129
1985	5.7	1.35	7.05	39,600	2,792	$1,186
1986	5.7	1.45	7.15	42,000	3,003	$1,251
1987	5.7	1.45	7.15	43,800	3,132	$1,320
1988	6.06	1.45	7.51	45,600**	3,425**	$1,459**
1989	6.06	1.45	7.51	48,000**	3,605**	$1,556**
1990	6.2	1.45	7.65	50,400**	3,856**	$1,683**
1991	6.2	1.45	7.65	53,700**	4,108**	$1,779**
1992 & After	6.2	1.45	7.65	Automatic Adjustments	—	—

*Beginning in 1984, the self-employed tax rate became essentially the same as the combined rate paid by workers and their employers. In 1984 only, an immediate tax credit of 0.3 percent of taxable wages was provided for OASDI contributions paid by employees. Similar credits for self-employed persons of 2.7, 2.3 and 2.0 percent are provided on OASDI and HI contributions on net earnings from self-employment in 1984, 1985, and 1986-1989 respectively. After 1989, self-employed persons will be allowed a federal income tax deduction equal to half of the combined OASDI and HI contribution they pay.
**Estimates based on *1986 Trustees Report*, alternative IIB after 1987.

The 1986 report on Social Security indicated that the combined trust funds of the cash programs (OASDI) are financially sound.

Although the program costs of the Supplementary Medical Insurance program are growing rapidly, SMI is actuarially sound because premiums and general revenue income are set to equal expenditures. Barring remedial legislation, however, Medicare's larger program, the Hospital Insurance program, will in all likelihood be exhausted at some point in the late-1990's. However, such legislation is virtually a certainty, since Congress, the President and the public will never allow the program to become insolvent.

Financing requires that yearly income to Social Security and

> The actuarial estimates... indicate that the assets of the Old-Age and Survivors Insurance (OASI) and Disability Insurance (DI) Trust Funds will be sufficient to permit the timely payment of OASDI benefits for many years into the future. The long-range 75-year estimates indicate that, under the intermediate assumptions, the OASDI program will experience about three decades of actuarial surpluses, with continuing actuarial deficits thereafter. The surpluses in the first part of the 75-year projection period approximately offset the later deficits, so that the program, as a whole, is said to be in close actuarial balance.
> —1986 Annual Report of the Trustees

Medicare should generally be sufficient to meet yearly obligations. Social Security's and Medicare's actuaries make careful estimates of anticipated income and program obligations. Not only do Social Security's actuaries project program revenues and expenditures in the cash programs over the short term (5-10 years), they also make careful long-term projections 75 years into the future.

Actuaries forecast the future financial status of the Social Security trust funds based on expected economic and demographic trends. Because no one really knows what economic or demographic changes will occur in the future, actuaries make several forecasts based on different sets of assumptions—optimistic, intermediate, and pessimistic. They differ according to what is assumed about such future trends as price increases, wage increases, unemployment, economic growth, labor force participation, birthrates, life expectancy, and immigration.

Basically, the short-term estimates concentrate on whether, over the next five years, there are enough revenues projected to meet anticipated program obligations. Social Security's actuaries also make 75-year projections of the financial status of the cash program by comparing anticipated program expenditures as a percent of all earnings subject to the payroll tax to anticipated revenues as a percent of taxable payroll. Coming up with a 75-year deficit or surplus expressed as a percent of taxable payroll is much more useful than dollar amounts because over 75 years the value of the dollar will change considerably.

Because the contours of the future are uncertain, long-term projections are subject to error and, in fact, to greater error the further out in time they go. OASDI program experience will, of course, not be precisely as estimated. Nevertheless, projections do provide useful indicators of probable experience 40, 50, 60, and up to 75 years in the future. They are useful to policymakers concerned with charting a stable course for Social Security's financing, and provide a reasonable basis for the mid-course corrections that are necessary from time to time.

Financial estimates for the HI program are made in much the same way as those for the cash programs. But these estimates are even more difficult to make because they also have to incorporate a variety of medical-cost assumptions (e.g., hospital and medical cost, average length of stay in hospitals, and hospital utilization rates). Medical costs, especially hospital costs, have been so volatile that it's very difficult to make accurate estimates even a year or two ahead.

SOCIAL SECURITY IS SECURE

Early in the 1980s, the news media were full of articles suggesting that Social Security might become bankrupt. Of course, it didn't and it won't. These reports ignored the fact that Social Security is too important to allow this to happen. The same is true of Medicare. These are the major institutions that protect against economic want in our country.

That there will be changes in Social Security and Medicare in the future, no one disputes. Significant changes were made in 1983, and more have occurred and will come. But Social Security and Medicare are two of the nation's most important achievements. A compassionate society requires a sound social insurance system as a way of enabling its citizens to protect themselves against basic risks. As long as our country is secure, Social Security will be secure.

SOCIAL SECURITY AND MEDICARE: PAST TO PRESENT

It's not a coincidence that nearly all developed countries have social insurance programs like Social Security and Medicare. The emergence of social insurance is tied to industrialization and economic growth. As societies industrialize, their economies grow and social protection against economic insecurity becomes more affordable.

Industrial societies are healthier than agricultural societies; improved nutrition, sanitation, and medical care enable both more people to reach old age and some people with severe disabilities to live. More people are dependent on the economy and must be protected against risks to their economic security.

Societies can tolerate only so much insecurity. Social insurance programs moderate economic insecurity, thus becoming a major source of political stability. And, Social Security and other pensions help underwrite a relatively new form of leisure—retirement—while also shifting some of the burden of unemployment from younger to older workers in exchange for a pension.

EARLY ORIGINS

Most European countries had established social insurance programs, primarily workers' compensation programs for workplace injuries, by the beginning of this century. Protection against other risks including old age, disability, death, unemployment, and health expenses usually followed.

Social reformers introduced the concept of social insurance in the United States early in the twentieth century, but relatively little progress was made before the 1930s. To some critics, social insurance was a foreign import, anathema to the American way of life. Americans were supposed to protect themselves through private effort. The family and private charity might serve as a backup and, if all else failed, some public largess might be available—most likely the county poorhouses or almshouses.

THE SOCIAL SECURITY ACT OF 1935

It took the depression of the 1930s and President Franklin Roosevelt's political leadership to gain passage of the Social Security Act. The time was right for social insurance. The Depression had shattered many arguments used against such a program: that individuals could protect themselves simply through personal savings and other private means; that the poor were lazy; and that private charities and local and state governments could provide adequately for needy individuals. On June 29, 1934, President Roosevelt signed the executive order establishing the cabinet-level Committee on Economic Security, charging it to develop a *comprehensive* social insurance plan.

Social insurance was a relatively new idea for the United States. Because including highly controversial programs like health and disability insurance in the initial package would have risked undermining political support, the committee recommended including only Unemployment Insurance—then called Unemployment Compensation—and Old-Age Insurance—then called Old-Age Benefits. But the committee made clear that these programs were the first steps of a comprehensive social insurance system.

The president signed the Social Security Act on August 14, 1935. In addition to Old-Age Insurance and Unemployment Insurance, it established grants to states for public assistance to the aged, the blind, and dependent children as well as for maternal and child health services, public health, crippled children services, child welfare, and vocational rehabilitation.

It's sometimes said that Social Security was originally designed to pay benefits in the same way as private insurance, that is, the value of benefits received should be identical to the value of contributions. Not so. Concern for providing adequate benefits for older workers and to low-income earners was part of the program from the very beginning. The benefit formula in the original act provided a higher return on past contributions to those with lower cumulative earnings. And, in 1939, the formula was further weighted to pay larger benefits to those reaching 65 in the early years of the program, who, because of their age, had not had much opportunity to contribute. Since 1935, the Social Security Act has expanded as President Roosevelt and other founders of the program intended, providing greater protection to more Americans.

PROGRAM CHANGES

Before Old-Age Insurance paid its first monthly benefits, major amendments were enacted in 1939, greatly increasing the program, adequacy. Protection was extended to certain survivors of covered workers as well as to wives and dependent children of retired workers. The date of payment of the first monthly Social Security benefits was moved up from January 1942 to January 1940, and, as noted, the benefit formula liberalized.

The next major amendments came in 1950. Eligibility criteria were broadened, coverage extended, and benefit levels increased roughly compensating for price increases since 1940.

The program continued to grow during the 1950s, adding disability insurance protection for persons over age 50, actuarially-reduced early retirement benefits for women, and widow's benefits at age 62 instead of 65. In 1960, disability insurance protection was extended to all covered workers under age 65. In the midst of a recession, Congress voted in 1961 to extend that option to retire early with reduced benefits to men aged 62 to 64, in large part to entice older workers out of the labor force and provide assistance to unemployed and ill older workers.

In 1965, Congress passed a health insurance program, Medicare, for covered persons aged 65 and over, to be extended later to long-term disabled persons and persons with permanent kidney failure. The 1965 amendments also established Medicaid, the public assistance program that finances health services for many low-income families and individuals.

Responding to concerns about high poverty rates among the aged (in 1967, 28.5 percent of persons 65 and over were officially defined as poor) and the desire to maintain the purchasing power of Social Security benefits, Congress enacted substantial benefit increases between 1968 and 1972.

And, in 1972, Congress decided to index benefits so that, beginning in 1975, benefits would be adjusted automatically to compensate for increases in the cost of living. The 1972 amendments also added a new public assistance program—Supplemental Security Income (SSI)—which guarantees a small income for needy aged, blind, and disabled persons.

FINANCING PROBLEMS OF SOCIAL SECURITY: 1975 TO 1983

During the mid-1970s and early 1980s attention shifted to concerns with Social Security's financing. Twice during this period, an adverse economy combined with the natural growth of the program's obligations to create short-term financing problems. In 1977 Congress passed, and President Carter signed, legislation which raised payroll taxes, reduced future benefits slightly, and corrected a shortcoming of the 1972 benefit formula which would, otherwise, result in a large long-term financing problem. All parties had reason to believe they had resolved the financing problems for at least the next 35 years. Unfortunately, before the ink was barely dry on the 1977 amendments, Social Security was, again, experiencing two financing problems—one short-term and the other long-term.

■ THE SHORT TERM PROBLEM

The short-term problem can be explained primarily by the economy's unexpected poor performance from 1978 through 1982. Social Security's short-term financing is very sensitive to economic events. Benefits increase as prices rise because of the automatic cost-of-living adjustments. Income increases primarily as prevailing wages grow in the economy. In normal times, wages increase more than inflation, with the result that more new revenues come in than go out as cost-of-living adjustments.

But the five years following the 1977 legislation were hardly "normal." For most of those years prices increased more than wages. In 1980, the worst year, the benefit increase was 14.3 percent, but wages went up only 9 percent. And, we also had very high rates of unemployment. In the absence of remedial legislation, Social Security benefits could not have been paid on time by late 1982. From 1983 to 1990, the total shortfall was estimated at roughly $75 billion. That's a lot of money, but relative to total program expenditures it was only about a 5 percent shortfall.

■ THE LONG-TERM PROBLEM

In 1982, the Social Security Trustees, based on their most commonly accepted intermediate assumptions, projected an average deficit of roughly 13 percent of anticipated expenditures from 1982 through 2056.

The cause of the long-term problem was primarily demographic. Once reaching age 65, Americans were living longer than in the past, and this trend was expected to continue. Though good news for most of us, this meant the program must pay benefits to the average retiree for a longer period of time.

Additionally, the anticipated growth of the population age 65 and over, especially as the "baby boom" generation reaches retirement age, was placing pressure on the program's financing. And, because families are smaller than they were in the 1950s and 1960s, relatively fewer workers would be available at about the same time the "baby boom" generation retires.

RESOLVING FINANCING PROBLEMS: THE 1983 AMENDMENTS

When President Reagan took office in 1981, it was clear that something would have to be done relatively soon to respond to the developing short-term financing problem. As for the long-term problem, that was less clear.

In March and May 1981, the administration put forth its own proposals, all but one involved reducing benefits including, for example, very large cuts in early retirement benefits for newly eligible retirees beginning in 1982. Altogether the president's proposals would have produced nearly twice as much long-term savings as was needed at the time—all from benefit reductions.

Strong reactions from senior citizen groups, labor, and representatives of both parties quickly followed the proposals. Congressman Claude Pepper stated that by "any calculation, the Administration has launched the most fundamental assault on the Social Security system since its inception 46 years ago." The president disavowed the May proposals which had caused the greatest uproar, and announced instead that he would set up a bipartisan commission to study Social Security's financing problems.

■ THE COMMISSION

The National Commission on Social Security Reform was composed of five members chosen by the President, five by the Republican congressional leadership, and five by the Democratic congressional leadership. This commission was very unusual. Its membership consisted of many of the key actors, both within and outside government, active in making Social Security policy. If *they* could agree, there was a good chance that Congress and the president would accept their agreement.

At the start some members were, like the president, clearly committed to a solution that relied exclusively on benefit cuts; others were committed to a solution relying primarily on expanding coverage and increasing taxes. Fortunately in the end, everyone gave a little.

Very significantly, the members of the commission agreed that Social Security's problems could be solved. Not only that, but this panel—composed of liberals, moderates, and conservatives—agreed that the the fundamental structure and principles of Social Security were sound and rejected ideas of creating a voluntary system, a fully funded system, or similar proposals that would radically change the program.

After months of negotiations, virtually at its final hour of existence in January 1983, a large and bipartisan majority of the commission signed a carefully balanced compromise that the White House and House Speaker Tip O'Neill had agreed to accept. No one liked every element of the package, which included an expansion of coverage, a small cut in the COLA, small short-term payroll tax increases, partial taxation of benefits of higher income beneficiaries, and increases in tax rates for self-employed people. However, acceptance of proposals which, by themselves, would be generally unacceptable became a reasonable price to pay within the context of a fair compromise.

Altogether, the compromise package met the short-term financing goal and solved about two-thirds of the projected long-term problem. The 12 members who signed onto the package "agreed to disagree" over what to do about the remaining third of the long-term problem.

■ CONGRESSIONAL ACTION

The legislation which followed, that Congress passed and the President signed, also included a provision that essentially raises the age of eligibility for full retirement benefits from 65 to 67 gradually over a 27-year period beginning in 2000. And it incorporated a cost containment provision which phased in an entirely new way of reimbursing hospitals under Medicare.

On June 24, 1983 the trustees of the Social Security program issued their annual report, saying that Social Security's combined Old-Age and Survivors Insurance and Disability Insurance Trust Funds are sound, both in the short run and the long run. And the financing of Social Security remains strong today.

Since 1983, there have been several smaller, but significant changes in Social Security and Medicare, especially in the Disability Insurance program. More will be said about these changes in the chapters that follow.

RECENT CHANGES IN SOCIAL SECURITY

Recent changes in Social Security will almost certainly have an effect on you and your family. Read this chapter very carefully.

THE 1983 AMENDMENTS

Although Social Security remains fundamentally the same, 1983's landmark legislation stabilized Social Security's financing and incorporated many changes for current and future beneficiaries and taxpayers. The major changes affecting Social Security are summarized in this chapter; less significant changes are described in the chapters that follow. As you read about them, keep in mind that the sacrifice some entail has been spread fairly evenly among different groups of citizens. The slight pain they cause most of us is probably a small price to pay for maintaining the financial stability of Social Security.

■ COST-OF-LIVING ADJUSTMENT CHANGES

Social Security beneficiaries took their share of the pain that went along with the compromise leading to the 1983 amendments. The new law delayed the June 1983 cost-of-living adjustment (COLA) and all future COLAs, by six months to December of each year (with the increased benefit payable in the January check). The 1972 amendments to the Social Security Act provided an automatic cost-of-living adjustment in June (payable in July) to begin in 1975 and to be "triggered" whenever the yearly increase in inflation was 3 percent or more. This automatic COLA isn't really a benefit increase. It simply maintains the purchasing power of benefits. This is one of the most important features of Social Security.

Although the 1983 amendments maintained the automatic COLA basically unchanged, as noted, future COLAs were delayed by six months. This change was expected to save about $39 billion by 1990 and to eliminate a significant chunk of the long-term financing problem projected at the time. Because the yearly cost-of-living adjustment is a very expensive aspect of Social Security, this was one logical place to pursue reduction in outlays.

How much is this change costing the typical beneficiary? To most it probably felt like a one-time delay in the COLA, from June 1983 (payable in the July check) to December 1983 (payable in January 1984), with annual COLAs resuming thereafter. The six-month delay in the 3.5 percent COLA amounted to a loss in 1983 of a bit less than $150 for the typical retired couple; about $84 for the typical single, retired worker.

Actually, the six-month delay occurs every year, for as long as the program continues. And so the change in the COLA actually represents roughly a 2 percent reduction in benefits.

Either way you look at this change, it's nothing to sneeze at. But relative to fears expressed by many in 1982 that Social Security might "go broke," it seems like a reasonable price to pay.

More recently, the Social Security cost-of-living adjustment has been a hotly debated topic in Congress. Under the press of large federal deficits, the Social Security COLA became a very tempting target for some members of Congress, particularly in the Senate where serious consideration was given to proposals to skip the 1986 COLA or otherwise limit the COLA over several years. Some members felt this way, in spite of the fact that Social Security is running large yearly surpluses; it is funded primarily by an ear-marked payroll tax, and cuts in Social Security would do virtually nothing to reduce the deficits in general revenues. These deficits were caused by the large tax cuts and increases in defense spending of the 1980's.

Ironically, when the dust settled, Congress passed major deficit reduction legislation in 1985 which exempted Social Security COLAs and benefits from the automatic cutbacks that might be required under the new legislation.

And then in 1986 Congress passed a law which essentially eliminated the 3 percent "trigger" for an automatic cost-of-living adjustment. To beneficiaries, this means that they will receive a COLA, beginning with their January 1987 check, whenever the yearly increase in inflation is 0.1 percent or more (after rounding). The 1987 COLA was 1.3 percent.

■ WILL MY BENEFITS BE TAXED?

Beginning in 1984, the new law makes up to one-half of Social Security benefits (and tier 1 Railroad Retirement) subject to taxation for beneficiaries whose incomes exceed certain base amounts—$25,000 for single taxpayers, $32,000 for married taxpayers filing jointly, $0 for married taxpayers living together at any point during the year and filing separately. These base amounts include your adjusted gross income plus half of your Social Security benefits plus certain nontaxable income such as interest from municipal bonds. The proceeds from taxable benefits are credited to the OASDI Trust Funds, increasing OASDI revenues by about $30 billion through 1990 and reducing the long-range deficit that was projected in 1982 by about one-third. Initially, this new provision affected only about 10 percent of all beneficiaries. Eventually, however, (30 or 40 years from now) price and wage growth will bring most incomes above the base amounts.

To determine whether you will pay taxes in 1987 on your Social Security income, first figure out which of the three base amounts applies to your situation—$25,000 for single taxpayers, $32,000 for married taxpayers filing jointly and $0 for married taxpayers living with their spouses at any point during the year and filing separately. The amount of your benefits subject to taxation will be the lesser of: one-half of your benefits or one-half of the amount by which your adjusted gross income, plus tax-exempt interest, plus one-half of your Social Security benefits exceeds the base amount that applies. The overwhelming majority of beneficiaries will not have incomes exceeding these base amounts, and their Social Security benefits will not be subject to taxation (see Table).

Each year the Social Security Administration sends beneficiaries Form 1099 to calculate whether a portion of their benefits will be counted as taxable income. For those who will pay taxes on their benefits, the additional tax they may need to pay can range from one dollar to perhaps three thousand dollars (in

WHO PAYS INCOME TAX ON THEIR SOCIAL SECURITY?

	Example 1 MARRIED ELDERLY COUPLE WITH ANNUAL SOCIAL SECURITY BENEFITS OF $10,000	Example 2 MARRIED ELDERLY COUPLE WITH ANNUAL SOCIAL SECURITY BENEFITS OF $11,000	Example 3 MARRIED ELDERLY COUPLE WITH ANNUAL SOCIAL SECURITY BENEFITS OF $12,000
1. Adjusted Gross Income (e.g. Wages plus rental income, plus taxable private pension income, plus taxable interest minus exclusions from income)	$26,000	$28,000	$54,000
2. Tax-Exempt Interest income (e.g. certain municipal bonds)	0	500	2,000
3. One-Half of All Social Security Benefits During the Year	5,000	5,500	6,000
4. Amount By Which Lines 1, 2 and 3, When Added, Exceed Base Amount ($32,000 for the couples in the examples)	$ 0	$ 2,000	$30,000
5. Amount of Social Security Income Reported as Taxable Income	$ 0	$ 1,000	$ 6,000

the case of very high-income beneficiaries who receive large monthly Social Security benefits). Most of these beneficiaries will pay approximately $800 in 1987. (Incidently, because the new tax reform law actually lowered overall tax rates, the amount of taxes that high-income beneficiaries pay on their Social Security benefits is also reduced.)

Taxation of benefits was one of the most important changes incorporated in the 1983 amendments. It is in keeping with the tax principle that income should be taxed at some point in life, either when earned or spent. And, it should be noted that, with the exception of a few cases of married persons who file taxes separately, not a single additional penny is being collected from persons who receive only Social Security benefits, or from low- or moderate-income beneficiaries.

■ HOW PAYROLL TAX CHANGES WILL AFFECT YOU

The 1983 amendments advanced previously scheduled payroll tax increases from 1985 to 1984, and part of an already scheduled 1990 tax increase to 1988. This change in the law was expected to bring in an additional $39 billion through 1989, but no additional yield thereafter, because the tax rate in 1990 and later has been left the same as it was under the old law.

How does this affect workers making payroll tax contributions through 1989? Average earners are expected to pay an additional $174 over this period—an average of $29 more per year. Those with incomes consistently above the taxable earnings ceiling are expected to pay approximately $450 extra—about $75 per year. These additional tax contributions by employees will also be matched by their employers.

■ WHAT ABOUT THE SELF-EMPLOYED?

The 1983 amendments corrected a long-standing inequity that gave advantages to self-employed persons, but disadvantages for everyone else. Since 1984, self-employed workers have essentially been treated like other workers. Prior to these changes, self-employed persons made contributions to the HI trust fund equal to one-half of the combined employee-employer rate, and contributions to the OASDI trust funds equal to about three-quarters of the combined employee-employer rate. Yet they received the same protection under the program as everyone else.

Besides equalizing the contribution rates of self-employed people, the new law also provided tax credits (2.7 percent in 1984, 2.3 percent in 1985, 2.0 percent in 1986-89) against the self-employment tax prior to 1990 and an income tax deduction comparable to one-half of the self-employed tax liability beginning in 1990. This results in self-employed people being treated more as businesses, which are allowed to deduct the payroll contributions they make for their employees as business expenses.

This change in tax treatment for self-employed persons was expected to increase OASDI revenues by $18 billion and HI revenues by $8 billion by 1990 and improve financing of Social Security and Medicare in the long run.

■ EXPANDING SOCIAL SECURITY COVERAGE

The 1983 amendments expanded coverage under the Social Security program. Beginning in 1984, new employees of the federal government were covered, making payroll tax contributions and earning the right to protection provided under the cash program (federal employees already made the full contribution to the HI Trust Fund since 1983, and military personnel have been covered since 1957). Also, as of January 1, 1984, coverage was extended to the president, vice-president, all members of Congress, most high-level political appointees, federal judges, and current employees of Congress who were not covered by the federal Civil Service Retirement System as of December 31, 1983. No longer is it true that the president and members of Congress do not contribute into the system.

Legislation passed in 1986 established a new Federal Employee's Retirement System (FERS) for the newly covered federal employees hired after January 1, 1984, and for those federal workers hired before 1984 who choose to join FERS during July through December 1987. FERS is a three-tier retirement system consisting of 1) Social Security, 2) a new federal employee pension plan and 3) a thrift savings plan.

Mandatory coverage was also extended beginning in 1984 to virtually all present and future employees of nonprofit organizations. In recent years, some nonprofits, especially hospitals, had stopped participating in the Social Security program as a cost-saving mechanism. Some others had never joined. Their employees, especially low-income and short-term employees, usually lost out. Comparable private pension coverage was provided only very rarely. This change protects employees of nonprofit organizations and increases the trust fund revenues.

The 1983 amendments prohibited states from terminating coverage of state and local government employees, and allowed previously withdrawn state and local groups to renew coverage. This, too, eliminates gaps in coverage for these employees, and increases revenues.

Altogether, the important extensions of coverage by the 1983 amendments were expected to provide increased revenues of $25 billion through 1989 and produce a substantial long-run savings, as well.

■ WILL THE RETIREMENT AGE BE RAISED?
The answer is yes if you were born in 1938 or later; no if born before 1938.

Age 65 is now the normal retirement age in Social Security, the age of eligibility for full benefits. Between 62 and 64, workers can accept reduced early retirement benefits: currently, for workers retiring at age 62, 80 percent of full benefits.

The 1983 amendments provided a gradual increase in the normal retirement age to begin in 2003. The new retirement age will be 66 for workers born in 1943 through 1954; 65 years and 10 months for those born in 1942; 65 years and 8 months for those born in 1941; etc. The normal retirement age will then be gradually raised to 67 for workers born in 1960 or later; to 66 and 10 months for those born in 1959, etc. Also, while maintaining age 62 as the earliest possible retirement age under Social Security, beginning in 2000 the benefit for early retirement at age 62 will be gradually changed from 80 percent of a full

WHEN CAN I RETIRE AND RECEIVE FULL BENEFITS?

YEAR OF BIRTH	ATTAINMENT OF AGE 62	AGE OF ELIGIBILITY FOR FULL BENEFITS: NORMAL RETIREMENT AGE (YEARS/MONTHS)	AGE 62 BENEFIT AS PERCENT OF BENEFITS AT NORMAL RETIREMENT AGE
1937 or earlier	1999 or earlier	65/0	80.0
1938	2000	65/2	79.2
1939	2001	65/4	78.3
1940	2002	65/6	77.5
1941	2003	65/8	76.7
1942	2004	65/10	75.8
1943-1954	2005-2016	66/0	75.0
1955	2017	66/2	74.2
1956	2018	66/4	73.3
1957	2019	66/6	72.5
1958	2020	66/8	71.7
1959	2021	66/10	70.8
1960 or later	2022 or later	67/0 and after	70.0

Source: Social Security Administration Public Information Circular

benefit to 70 percent by 2022. This provision reduced the long-run deficit that was projected in 1982 by about one-third.

What does this mean for younger workers? First, those who must wait until age 66 to receive full benefits will experience a benefit reduction, the equivalent, on average, of about 6 percent, because they will have to wait longer to get full benefits. Those who must wait until 67 will experience the equivalent of a 13 percent reduction. Unfortunately, the loss in benefits will be greatest for those who must retire at earlier ages due to health problems or unemployment. Widows and widowers and spouses subject to the new retirement age, too, will experience similar benefit reductions. On the other hand, because life expectancies at age 65 have generally increased since Social Security was first enacted and can be expected to continue to do so, those affected by this change will generally receive Social Security benefits for more years than earlier beneficiaries did.

RECENT CHANGES IN SOCIAL SECURITY AND SSI DISABILITY PROGRAMS

The 1980s have been a very turbulent period in the administration of the Social Security Disability Insurance (DI) and SSI disability programs. They have been administered in a manner that has been unfair to hundreds of thousands severely disabled Americans and their families. As you read about the changes which have occurred, keep in mind that the situation has improved mainly because Congress, the federal court system, and many state governments have stopped some of the most unfair and harsh aspects of the programs' administration.

During the mid-1970s, the Social Security disability rolls were growing very rapidly, adding about 500,000 to 600,000 workers per year who applied for benefits. The number of disability awards Social Security made per year crept up from a little fewer than 5 per 1000 protected workers during the late 1960s to as high as 7.1 per 1000 in 1975. (Since 1980, the numbers of new awards dipped to as low as 2.9 per 1000 in 1982.)

■ THE 1980 DISABILITY AMENDMENTS

Responding to concerns about the growth of the disability rolls, the disability program began to be tightened during the Carter administration. Congress passed the 1980 Disability Amendments, designed to increase work incentives for disabled persons and also to tighten the administration of the Social Security and SSI disability programs to ensure that benefits go only to individuals who met the disability criteria—that is, not to those who have recovered or perhaps were never really disabled. Also, the 1980 law reduced benefits for disabled workers under 47 and to those with families. The 1981 law made further cuts to those receiving other public benefits.

The 1980 amendments required that, beginning in 1982, the disability status of nonpermanently disabled workers be reviewed at least every third year. Continuing disability reviews (CDRs) of people receiving disability benefits were already being made, but not at the rates mandated under the 1980 amendments, and generally only in the first year or two after award. The amendments also reduced the value of benefits for the families of some disabled workers and incorporated new incentives for the rehabilitation of disabled workers (see Chapter 10).

Citing a General Accounting Office (GAO) study suggesting that as many as 20 percent of the disabled should not be on the rolls, the Reagan administration sped up the new review process, beginning it in March 1981 instead of 1982. Ironically, as the House Aging Committee pointed out, the study the administration cited was later criticized because 40 percent of the disability beneficiaries originally found "not disabled" were, in fact, disabled when the Social Security Administration doublechecked. The periodic reviews began and between March 1981 and April 1984 nearly 1,200,000 DI and SSI disability cases were reviewed. The results were that initially almost 500,000 people were terminated from the disability rolls along with family members, about 42 percent of all cases reviewed. (Many were later reinstated on appeal).

Congressman Claude Pepper, Democratic chairman of the House Rules Committee, referred to these terminations as "nothing less than a wholesale purge of the disability rolls," suggesting that the administration was seeking to obtain—through the backdoor—budgetary savings that had been denied when its 1981 disability proposals were rejected. Senator John Heinz III, then Republican Chairman of the Senate Aging Committee, called the disability reviews "a holocaust against the mentally impaired." Newspapers reported suicides related to removal from the program and cited startling examples of highly questionable decisions to terminate benefits.

The implementation of this review process was hasty, resulting in great strain on the already overburdened state agencies that make the initial disability determinations. In effect, the periodic review process required that beneficiaries prove once again they are disabled. Because of poor notification, many beneficiaries and their physicians did not realize that lack of medical improvement was insufficient for continuance of benefits. Although there was no legislative tightening of the definition of disability, as a result of administrative changes some beneficiaries were being evaluated under stricter criteria than those that prevailed when they first applied for disability benefits. In fact, even the Supreme Court noted in a unanimous 1986 decision, "Bowen versus the State of New York," that SSA had surreptitiously changed disability eligibility criteria for mentally disabled persons so as to illegally restrict eligibility.

Persons denied benefits because of the periodic reviews can ask for reconsideration and then appeal to administrative law judges (ALJ). There was a very high rate of reversal at the ALJ level of initial decisions to terminate benefits, averaging over 60 percent in 1981 through 1983. One reason for this high reversal rate is that the ALJs continued to be governed by the Social Security Act and federal regulations and rulings that reflected Congress's intent, whereas the procedures issued to govern the state agencies making disability evaluations were, as the American Association of Retired Persons (AARP) put it, "often at variance with the standards set forth in the Social Security Act, Regulations and Rulings." Another reason was that cases most likely to be reversed are brought to the ALJ level.

Initially, benefits were often terminated immediately if the periodic review found a person no longer disabled. Return of payments sometimes was sought for all months from the date the disability was determined to have ceased. Even if a decision was appealed, the person's payments would be stopped.

In short, by late 1983 the administration of the reviews was a mess, resulting in numerous law suits, including two class action suits that found SSA guilty of implementing a surreptitious and illegal policy discriminating against the mentally ill. Also, according to the House Aging Committee, at least 21 states refused in whole or in part to administer the disability reviews and 25 federal courts struck down SSA's internal operating procedures and ordered the reopening of many decisions.

■ CHANGES IN 1983, 1984

Responding to public concern, some changes were made. Legislation was enacted in January 1983 and SSA also initiated some reforms. Some of the changes that are still in effect require:

- that state disability review agencies offer a hearing at which evidence be evaluated and that the terminated beneficiary be given the opportunity to appear at such a hearing;
- that terminated beneficiaries be given better notification of the reconsideration procedures and their right to appeal;
- face-to-face interviews at local Social Security offices at the start of each continuing disability review;
- an expansion of the definition of the "permanently disabled" so as to exempt more persons from the review;
- mandating that a disability "ceases" when the beneficiary is notified of termination so that he or she generally will not be subject to recoupment of past benefits.

■ THE DISABILITY BENEFITS REFORM ACT OF 1984

Despite these reforms, support built for more substantial changes in the disability review process. One factor was a GAO report that showed that the review guidelines subjected the mentally impaired to much harder eligibility criteria than were other disabled people. Another factor was concern that clear medical improvement be a criterion for terminations of benefits. The result: Congress passed the Disability Benefits Reform Act of 1984 by a vote of 402 to 0 in the House and 99 to 0 in the Senate. The act included the following provisions:

- a medical improvement standard ensuring that benefits could be terminated only if substantial evidence showed that the recipient's medical condition had improved;
- a requirement that the combined effects of multiple impairments be taken into consideration when making eligibility decisions;
- a moratorium on mental health reviews until implementation of new mental impairment standards;

- new standards for obtaining and using medical evidence;
- a requirement that a careful study be made on how the evaluation of allegations of pain by individuals should be used to determine eligibility for benefits.

Since enactment of this new law, SSA has been busy implementing these procedures. Working with mental health professionals, new mental health impairment standards have been issued, enabling CDRs for mentally impaired persons to begin again in 1986. Medical improvement standards and new medical criteria for determining eligibility were also issued in December 1985. CDRs resumed in January 1986.

Has the Disability Benefits Reform Act of 1984 reduced the inequities and hardships brought about by the over-zealous implementation of the 1980 Disability Amendments? The answer is a qualified "yes." How much, however, remains to be seen and will depend in large part on whether SSA and the administration adhere to the spirit of the law.

■ OTHER RECENT CHANGES
Other recent changes may affect you, too.

New Checks—In late 1985, the United States Treasury began issuing *all* government checks on the same colored, counterfeit-resistant paper. The only difference now between Social Security and SSI checks is that Social Security checks come in khaki-colored envelopes and SSI in pale blue envelopes.

New Social Security Cards—Since October 1983, all new and replacement Social Security cards have been issued on counterfeit-resistant banknote paper.

Food Stamp Applications—Beginning in 1986, Social Security offices provide information about food stamps and applications to persons receiving and applying for Social Security. SSA is not, however, required to take applications for food stamps, except from certain SSI recipients.

Recoupment of Benefits—In cases in which 1) Social Security and SSI funds are electronically transferred into joint accounts;

> I agree that individuals who are not eligible should be removed from the rolls; however, the administration's implementation of the reviews brought emotional and financial hardship to thousands of truly disabled. Let us hope that the actions of the Congress, the courts, and the states have rectified the problems.
> Congressman Edward R. Roybal,
> Chairman, House Committee on Aging
> in a letter in the September 11, 1985
> *Wall Street Journal.*

2) one party dies; and 3) the other party (parties) is (are) entitled to benefits based on the deceased person's earnings record, SSA must give adequate notice of intent to recoup overpayments. It must also allow the surviving joint account holder(s) opportunity to appeal this decision, to request a waiver, or to repay gradually.

Still other changes—will be discussed in the chapters that follow.

Applying For Benefits

If you need specific information about your benefits under the Social Security programs, contact your local Social Security office. You'll find knowledgeable employees whose purpose is to give you the best and most up-to-date information, and to help process claims.

About 1320 local Social Security offices—covering every state, the District of Columbia, Puerto Rico, the Virgin Islands, and more—and 3400 small contact stations—for rural and isolated communities—handle old-age, survivors, disability, and Medicare applications and SSI applications, as well. Social Security publishes many free, useful pamphlets and provides much information and service by telephone through their 34 teleservice centers. Often a claim can be processed by telephone, so to save time, call before going into your local office. The number is listed under "Social Security" in your telephone directory. When you call, have your Social Security card in front of you, so you can give the staff your number.

The next few chapters provide an overview of benefits. Do not consider this summary a substitute for contacting Social Security. The Social Security program is complex and, as you have seen, important changes are sometimes made in the program over the course of the year. Everything you need to know will not necessarily be covered in this book. And, always check and double-check your information.

YOUR SOCIAL SECURITY NUMBER

You need your Social Security number, which appears on your Social Security card, to receive credit for your contributions to Social Security and, later, to apply for benefits. Getting a Social Security card is a simple procedure. Applications are accepted at any Social Security office. If you are under age 18, you can apply by mail, telephone, or in person. If 18 or older and applying for your first Social Security card, you must go to a local Social Security office. (This, however, will not be happening very much in the future because the new tax reforms require that, beginning in 1987, parents apply for Social Security cards for all children aged five or over.) If you change your name (e.g., by marrying) be sure to apply for a duplicate card. You'll need to provide evidence of your old and new names. Also, be sure to apply for a replacement if you lose your card. An official birth certificate or baptismal certificate is generally the best identification when applying for a Social Security card.

HOW TO APPLY FOR BENEFITS

To receive benefits, you must apply for them. The Social Security Administration says you should contact a local office if:

- you're unable to work due to illness or injury that is expected to last 12 or more months or result in death;
- you're about to be 62 or older and are planning to retire;
- you're a few months away from your 65th birthday. Even if you're not planning to retire, you should contact Social Security about your Medicare benefits, which are available regardless of whether you retire;
- there's a death in your family;
- someone in your family suffers permanent kidney failure.

Plan ahead. You may apply three months before you want your retirement benefits to begin. To help speed along your application, be sure to bring along these three most important items:

- your Social Security card and, in certain cases, the card of each member of your immediate family;
- your W-2 forms for at least the last two years or, if self-employed, your last two federal tax returns;

- birth certificates for you and each member of the family for whom you are applying for benefits. If you don't have a birth certificate, other official certificates that prove age will probably do.

In certain cases, additional items may be needed. For example, if applying for spouse, widow's, or widower's benefits, bring a marriage certificate; if applying for disability benefits, supply names, addresses, and telephone numbers of doctors and medical institutions treating your disability.

If you're not well enough to get to a Social Security office, you can still apply. First, try calling your local Social Security office. If a personal interview is necessary, tell them about your situation. They should send a representative to interview you in your home.

Sometimes a beneficiary (for example, a young child under 18 or a severely mentally retarded person) is unable to manage personal finances. In that case, checks can be sent to a relative or some other person called a "representative payee," who takes on significant responsibilities such as accounting for the use of funds and reporting changes in the status of a beneficiary that might affect his or her benefits.

CAN I APPEAL AN ELIGIBILITY DECISION?

You can appeal Social Security decisions, but you almost always need to make this appeal within 60 days—and sometimes sooner—of the day you receive written notice from Social Security of a decision. The first step in the appeals process is to ask, in writing, for reconsideration of your claim. If the results of the reconsideration are not satisfactory, you may request a hearing before an administrative law judge. Next you may appeal to the Social Security Administration's Appeals Council. If the outcome is still unsatisfactory, you may file a suit in federal court. You may be represented by a lawyer or other person of your choice when appealing. Also, if appealing a decision that you are no longer sufficiently disabled to receive disability benefits, you have the right to meet with a disability hearing officer to state your case if the person who reviews your reconsideration recommends discontinuance of benefits. After that, you can continue your appeal, if necessary, to the administrative law judge level. Also, if you are appealing this type of decision to terminate disability benefits, through 1987 you may choose to continue receiving monthly benefits and Medicare coverage (if you have it) usually through the reconsideration and the administrative law judge levels. But you must make a written request within ten days of receiving each decision to terminate benefits. If you lose your appeal, you may have to repay these benefits (except Medicare), although it is also possible to request a waiver of repayment.

Persistence often pays off. If you think you or a member of your family has been wrongly denied benefits, especially disability benefits, be sure to appeal. By the way, your local Social Security Office has a useful pamphlet entitled *Your Right to Question the Decision Made on Your Social Security Claim*.

WHAT ARE MY RESPONSIBILITIES?

In two other free pamphlets, *Your Social Security Rights and Responsibilities—Retirement and Survivors Benefits* and *Your Social Security Rights and Responsibilities—Disability Benefits*, the Social Security Administration details certain things that covered workers and Social Security beneficiaries or their families should report. Everyone must report change of mailing address, change of name, work outside the United States, and loss of Social Security card. Beneficiaries and their families are required to report earnings above the annual limit or work by a disabled beneficiary, a trip outside the United States for 30 days or more, divorce or annulment, marriage, birth or adoption of a child, death of a beneficiary, inability of a beneficiary to manage funds, that a child nearing 16 or 18 is disabled or a full-time primary or secondary student, and that such a beneficiary (age 18, or, in a few cases, 19) is no longer a full-time student. Also, contact SSA if you lose your Social Security or SSI check or do not receive your check by the 7th of the month.

DIRECT DEPOSIT OF YOUR BENEFITS

You can arrange to have your monthly Social Security or SSI check deposited directly into a checking or savings account rather than being mailed to your home. You can get a direct deposit form from your bank, credit union, or savings and loan association. This may be quicker and more convenient for you.

IF MORE HELP IS NEEDED

The local office and the teleservice centers are equipped to handle public inquiries about Social Security, routine and otherwise. You should always call them first and try to work with them on solving any problems. If all else fails, you might want to pay for a long distance call to the Office of Public Inquiries at the National Headquarters of the Social Security Administration; the number is 301-594-7700.

Also, under certain circumstances, you may want to seek legal advice from a legal assistance program or private lawyer; get a referral and advice from a social service agency or senior center; or call the office of a member of Congress.

RECENT ADMINISTRATIVE CHANGES

You should know about certain changes in the administration of Social Security that may affect you when applying for benefits.

Computer Modernization—Although Social Security once had a state-of-the-art computer system, inadequate updating of the system had caused it to deteriorate to the point of seriously jeopardizing the administration of the program. Fortunately, significant improvements have been made in the computer system during the past few years. The result is that local offices now are generally able to get the information needed for processing claims much faster than in the past and the SSA's ability to perform important functions like recording earnings histories of covered workers and calculating changes in benefits is improving. Assuming adequate staffing and continued progress in updating and automating the system, service to the public is likely to be better in the future. Even with improvements, for the roughly 5 percent of cases that are particularly complex, there remains a need for staff to help the public cut through "red tape".

SSA Staff Reductions—Nationwide, in 1983 SSA employed 87,000 people, mostly in local offices, assisting beneficiaries and prospective beneficiaries. The numbers of employees declined to about 78,000 in mid-1986, with plans by the Reagan administration for further reductions to about 61,000 by 1990. Workloads are lower than ever, processing times faster, and the administration anticipates further efficiencies from increased automation. Those favoring staff reductions believe service to the public will continue to improve and the taxpayer will save money. Some disagree, suggesting that these changes are being made with very little regard for service to the public, that SSA workloads are going down, in part because of reduced outreach, and that these reductions are likely to lead to large scale closings of local offices. And they point out that such changes are not prudent given the anticipated growth in the number of elderly persons and the fact that SSA's own internal study recommended that systems modernization should result in a reduction of 5,700 jobs by 1990, not 17,000.

It remains to be seen whether such large-scale cuts will be made and, if they are, what the effect will be on service to the public.

DETERMINING YOUR BENEFIT AMOUNTS

Your payroll tax contributions are not deposited into a savings account at Social Security with your name on it. Instead, they go to the OASI, DI, and HI Trust Funds, used primarily to pay benefits to current beneficiaries. But, don't worry, indirectly you do receive credit for your contributions. A record of all your earnings in covered employment is maintained and updated regularly at Social Security.

For you and your family to be eligible for benefits, you need to earn credit for a certain amount of work under the program. You earn these credits, "quarters of coverage," through your payroll tax contributions. During the course of a year, you can earn up to four quarters of coverage.

In 1987 workers receive a quarter of coverage for each $460 earned in a job covered by Social Security. (The amount of covered earnings needed to earn a quarter of coverage goes up each year in tandem with increases in average wages.) In general, employers report and make contributions on all the covered earnings of their covered employees up to the maximum taxable ceiling. However, there are some exceptions. For example, earnings from self-employment count, in some cases, even if your net profit is less than $400 in a calendar year.

You may well ask whether, if you need to earn only $460 for each quarter of coverage in 1987 and if you can only earn four quarters in a year, it pays for you to make contributions on more than $1840 of covered earnings? The answer is almost always yes. The more you contribute, the more you are likely to get.

WHEN AM I ELIGIBLE FOR BENEFITS?

Eligibility for benefits generally requires that the worker on whose earnings history benefits are being claimed be either "fully insured," "currently insured," or "disability insured." Eligibility can be established for all benefits (except disabled worker benefits) if fully insured. To achieve fully insured status, you generally need one quarter of coverage for each year after 1950 or, if later, for each year after age 21 and before reaching age 62, or dying, or becoming disabled before age 62. You need at least 6 quarters of coverage, but never more than 40.

Some survivors' benefits (for example, childrens', lump-sum payment) can be paid if a worker is currently insured, that is, if the worker has at least six quarters of coverage in the 13-quarter period (roughly three years) before his or her death.

Besides being fully insured, a worker (unless disabled by blindness) needs to be "disability insured" to qualify for disability benefits. Disabled workers aged 31 or older need credit for 20 out of the last 40 quarters (ten years) prior to onset of their disability. If disabled before age 31, workers can alternatively have quarters equal to half the total quarters since they were 21 and before they became disabled. If under age 24, they need at least six quarters out of the last 12 quarters.

THE PIA—THE BASIS OF ALL BENEFITS

Benefits are generally defined as a certain percent of the primary insurance amount, or PIA. What does that mean? The language associated with how benefit levels are determined is, as you have already read, highly specialized. Let's demystify this.

Think of the primary insurance amount, PIA, as the benefit you are entitled to if you retire at the normal retirement age

IF YOU ARE 62 IN	NUMBER OF QUARTERS OF COVERAGE NEEDED TO QUALIFY FOR RETIREMENT BENEFITS
1983	32
1984	33
1985	34
1986	35
1987	36
1988	37
1991 or later	40

(now 65). This benefit equals 100 percent of the PIA. Social Security's benefit formula translates lifetime earnings in jobs covered by Social Security into a worker's PIA. We'll discuss that formula next. But first, take a look at the chart on the next page which summarizes the basic insured status requirements and the current percent of PIA's for the major cash benefits.

HOW THE BENEFIT FORMULA WORKS

Several Social Security benefit formulas exist, but the formula widely used for workers reaching age 62 in 1979 and later is called the "wage-indexed method." This method is designed to ensure that Social Security reflects changes in the prevailing wages over a person's lifetime. Most of us want to maintain our prior standard of living in retirement. Experts suggest our retirement income needs to replace between 60 and 80 percent of pre-retirement income. (Lower taxes on retirement income and certain reduced expenses make replacing 100 percent of pre-retirement income unnecessary.) Social Security assists us in doing this by guaranteeing a pension that bears a relatively constant relationship to our pre-retirement standard of living. For example, workers, young and old, with average wages throughout their worklife can count on Social Security replacing about 41 percent of their pre-retirement income if they retire at the normal retirement age (not 65).

To compute your PIA, you must first figure out what your average earnings were on jobs in which you contributed to Social Security. This is called your Average Indexed Monthly Earnings (AIME). We'll talk about how you get your AIME in a second. For now let's assume you know what it is. Once the AIME is figured out, the following formula is used to get your PIA:

For workers who reach 62 or become disabled in 1986:

1. the first $297 of the AIME is multiplied by 90 percent;
2. then the next $1493 of the AIME is multiplied by 32 percent;
3. any remainder of the AIME is multiplied by 15 percent;
4. and, then the results are summed. This is the PIA.

TYPE OF MONTHLY BENEFIT	INSURED STATUS REQUIREMENT	PERCENT OF PIA (1983-1999)
Retirement at:		
Age 70	Fully Insured	115*
Age 65	Fully Insured	100
Age 62	Fully Insured	80
Disabled Worker under 65	Fully Insured and Disability Insured	100
BENEFITS FOR FAMILY MEMBERS OF RETIRED AND DISABLED WORKERS:**		
Spouse Age 65+	Worker Entitled	50
Spouse Age 62+	Worker Entitled	37½
Mothers, Fathers, Children, Disabled Child 18 or over	Worker Entitled	50
SURVIVORS:**		
Widow(er) at Age 65++	Worker Fully Insured	100
Widow(er) at Age 60++	Worker Fully Insured	71½
Dependent Parents Age 62)	Worker Fully Insured	82½
Disabled Widow(er) Age 50-59	Worker Fully Insured	71½
Disabled Child 18 or Older	Worker Fully or Currently Insured	75
Mothers, Fathers, Children	Worker Fully or Currently Insured	75

*Will be slightly higher for those attaining age 70 after 1995 because of 1983 amendments.
**Generally subject to maximum family benefit limitations and deductions for earnings.
+Same benefits generally available to divorced spouses who were married 10 years or longer.
++Same benefits available to divorced widows or widowers who were married 10 years or longer.

Each year the formula's dollar amounts are changed to keep up with average wages. This is one of the ways that replacement rates are held constant. For workers reaching 62 in 1985, the first $280 of the AIME was multiplied by 90 percent, the next $1411 by 32 percent and the excess by 15 percent. For those reaching 62 in 1984, the first $267 was multiplied by 90 percent, the next $1345 by 32 percent and the excess by 15 percent.

Let's figure out the PIAs and approximate Social Security replacement rates of three workers who reach age 62 in 1986. Bill has earned minimum wages all his life. Mary has been an average income earner, and John has always had (See table below.) earnings at the Social Security earnings ceiling each year.

As these examples illustrate, the formula replaces a higher proportion of prior earnings for low-income earners like Bill, but provides larger dollar benefits for high-income earners like John. Because most people claim benefits early, accepting permanently reduced benefits, actual replacement rates are smaller. Also, in case you are wondering, one reason that Bill's replacement rate is unusually high is that the federal minimum wage has not been raised from $3.35 an hour since 1981.

COMPUTING YOUR AIME

Now that you understand the significance of the PIA and how the benefit formula translates your AIME into the PIA, let's compute the AIME.

First, consider what the indexing procedure does. It updates past earnings on a worker's earnings history to compensate for changes in average wages. Without this procedure dollars earned early in one's career, when wages were much lower, would be given the same weight as dollars earned near retirement. This would result in lower average wages over the course

WORKER	AIME	(90% OF $297)	+	(32% OF NEXT $1,493)	+	(15% OF EXCESS)	=	PIA*	REPLACEMENT RATE**
Bill	$ 713	$267.30	+	$133.12	+	0	=	$400.40	69%
Mary	$1346	$267.30	+	$335.68	+	0	=	$602.90	43%
John	$2078	$267.30	+	$477.76	+	$43.20	=	$788.20	24%

*PIAs are rounded down to the lower 10 cents.
** One way Social Security replacement rates for retired workers are calculated is by dividing the PIA by the earnings subject to payroll taxes in the year before the beneficiary reaches reaches age 62.

of a career than under the procedure. For instance, average wages in 1951 were about $2800. A worker who earned $3200 in 1951 was doing fairly well relative to the standard of the day. Under the AIME procedure, such a worker reaching 62 in 1986 would receive credit for about $18,560 in in 1951. Here's why.

Under the indexing procedure, the indexing year is defined as two years before the retiree reaches age 62. The indexing year for our friend who reached 62 in 1986 would be 1984. Every year prior to 1984 back through 1951 is updated to compensate for the increase in average wages that have occurred between that year and 1984. So, for instance, since average wages in 1984 were roughly 5.8 times greater than average wages in 1951, you simply multiply the earnings in covered employment in 1951 times 5.8. (In the case of our friend, 5.8 times $3,200 equal $18,560.*) You would repeat the procedure for 1952 and so on for each year up to 1984.

The number of years used in calculating the AIME for retired workers equals the number of years *after 1950 (or age 21 if later)* and *before* the worker reaches age 62. The five lowest years of earnings (after indexing)—or non-earnings as the case may be—are dropped out. (Unindexed earnings after age 62 can be used if they are high earnings years.) Then the earnings (indexed or otherwise) are added together and divided by the number of months in the number of years used in calculating the AIME. The result is the AIME. Once you have the AIME, you can compute the PIA using the formula we reviewed, which gives a pretty good idea of the value of potential benefits.

The next page has a worksheet put out by Social Security. You may use this to estimate your benefits if you reach age 62 in 1983, 1984, 1985, or 1986. In column A, you'll find the maximum taxable earnings covered by Social Security for each year since 1951. In column B, enter all your earnings since 1951. Enter zero for no earnings, and do not enter more than the maximum taxable earnings in any year. The indexing factors you

---

*The indexing factor is figured to seven decimal places in the Social Security benefit formula. Consequently, this worker's 1951 earnings would actually be indexed to $18,445.61 (5.7642543 x $3,200).

WORKSHEET

			YOU REACH 62 IN			
YEAR	A	B	C 1983*	C 1984*	C 1985*	C 1986*	D
1951	$ 3,600	—	4.9	5.2	5.4	5.8	—
1952	3,600	—	4.6	4.9	5.2	5.4	—
1953	3,600	—	4.4	4.6	4.9	5.1	—
1954	3,500	—	4.4	4.6	4.8	5.1	—
1955	4,200	—	4.2	4.4	4.6	4.9	—
1956	4,200	—	3.9	4.1	4.3	4.6	—
1957	4,200	—	3.8	4.0	4.2	4.4	—
1958	4,200	—	3.7	4.0	4.1	4.4	—
1959	4,800	—	3.6	3.8	4.0	4.2	—
1960	4,800	—	3.4	3.6	3.8	4.0	—
1961	4,800	—	3.4	3.6	3.7	3.9	—
1962	4,800	—	3.2	3.4	3.6	3.8	—
1963	4,800	—	3.1	3.3	3.5	3.7	—
1964	4,800	—	3.0	3.2	3.3	3.5	—
1965	4,800	—	3.0	3.1	3.3	3.5	—
1966	6,600	—	2.8	2.9	3.1	3.3	—
1967	6,600	—	2.6	2.8	2.9	3.1	—
1968	7,800	—	2.5	2.6	2.7	2.9	—
1969	7,800	—	2.3	2.5	2.6	2.7	—
1970	7,800	—	2.2	2.3	2.5	2.6	—
1971	7,800	—	2.1	2.2	2.3	2.5	—
1972	9,000	—	1.9	2.0	2.1	2.3	—
1973	10,800	—	1.8	1.9	2.0	2.1	—
1974	13,200	—	1.7	1.8	1.9	2.0	—
1975	14,100	—	1.6	1.7	1.8	1.9	—
1976	15,300	—	1.5	1.6	1.6	1.7	—
1977	16,500	—	1.4	1.5	1.6	1.6	—
1978	17,700	—	1.3	1.4	1.4	1.5	—
1979	22,900	—	1.2	1.3	1.3	1.4	—
1980	25,900	—	1.1	1.2	1.2	1.3	—
1981	29,700	—	1.0	1.1	1.1	1.2	—
1982	32,400	—	1.0	1.0	1.0	1.1	—
1983	35,700	—	1.0	1.0	1.0	1.1	—
1984	37,800	—	1.0	1.0	1.0	1.0	—
1985	39,600	—	1.0	1.0	1.0	1.0	—
1986	42,000	—	1.0	1.0	1.0	1.0	—
1987	43,800*	—	1.0	1.0	1.0	1.0	—
TOTAL					$		

*Indexing factors in this table are carried out to the nearest tenth, whereas those in the actual benefit formula are actually carried out to many places.
Source: Social Security Administration Pamphlet, "Estimating Your Social Security Retirement Check Using the Indexing Method" (January, 1983 Edition).

should use, depending on the year you reached age 62, are listed in column C. Multiply the amounts you put in column B times the indexing factor for each year.

If you were 62 in 1983, you want to select the 27 highest years of earnings on your list; if 62 in 1984, the 28 highest years, etc. Add up all these years and divide by the number of appropriate months. This gives your AIME at age 62. This, in turn, is plugged into the Social Security benefit formula to give your PIA. The PIA is, generally, updated for inflation each year.

The PIA for deceased and disabled workers is calculated in a similar manner, though fewer years are generally used.

If you still want to estimate your benefits, call Social Security and ask them to send their pamphlets on estimating benefits and the form you need to fill out to get a free record of earnings credited to your Social Security account.

Remember, this is a rough estimate. Workers who reached age 62 in 1979 through 1983 actually had benefits calculated in at least two ways. They receive benefits based on the more favorable calculation, usually the one based on this indexing procedure. Also, other factors, may affect the calculation. For example, if you served in the military, you may receive wage credits on your earnings history that increase your PIA.

Further, factors such as early retirement, delaying your retirement past normal retirement age, earnings while receiving your benefits, and receipt of a pension based on work that was not covered by Social Security, may affect the size of your benefits. But the chapters that follow discuss this further.

RETIREMENT BENEFITS

Workers who have contributed into Social Security for enough years earn both retirement and family benefits and have considerable choice over the timing of their retirement.

WHEN CAN I RETIRE?

Social Security provides what in reality amounts to a continuum of retirement ages, currently ranging from 62 to 70. Before you decide to receive benefits, it's important to know the choices you have.

Normal Retirement Benefit. If you were born before 1938, you will be eligible for unreduced retirement benefits, 100 percent of the primary insurance amount, at age 65. The normal retirement age will increase gradually to age 67 between 2003 and 2027, with increased reductions for early retirement phasing in gradually beginning in 2000 (see Chapter 5).

Early Retirement Benefit. Most retirees actually begin receiving benefits before age 65. If you were born before 1938 and retire early (that is, claim benefits early), your benefit is permanently reduced 5/9 of 1 percent for each month of retirement before your 65th birthday. That works out to a benefit of 80 percent if you claim benefits before 2000 at the earliest possible age, 62.

Delayed Retirement Benefit. For those reaching 65 from 1982 through 1989, the ultimate benefit is increased by 1/4 of a percent for each month benefits are not received after normal retirement age (up to the age of 70). That's 3 percent a year. So, if you delay your retirement all the way to age 70, your benefit would be increased to 115 percent of your PIA. For people reaching 65 prior to 1982, the delayed retirement credit was 1/12 percent a month, or 1 percent a year. The 1983 amendments gradually increase the delayed retirement credit beginning in 1990; the increase will rise to 8 percent per year for workers who delay their retirement past normal retirement ages in 2009 and later.

Currently, if you retire after age 65, you may be able to receive retroactive benefits for as much as six months (subject to the earnings test), although generally not for as far back as the time before you reached 65.

SPECIAL BENEFITS

Special Minimum Benefit. This benefit, an alternative way of computing the PIA, is designed to help workers who have worked consistently, but at low wages, in jobs covered by Social Security. For monthly benefits payable after 1986 the PIA for the special minimum can be approximated by multiplying the number of years of coverage in excess of 10 and up to 30 by $19.29. The amount is increased each year by the COLA.

The Minimum Benefit. This benefit, which provides a minimum PIA of $122 plus COLAs, is being phased out. People currently receiving it will continue to do so. Only a few people who were eligible prior to 1981 but did not file, plus certain members of religious orders who have taken a vow of poverty and are covered by Social Security, are still eligible to start receiving it.

Special Benefits for Those Aged 72 or Older Before 1968. Certain individuals who reached age 72 before 1968 are eligible for a special benefit even if they never contributed to Social Security, as are some workers (and their spouses) who reached age 72 shortly after 1968 with relatively few quarters of coverage.

BENEFITS FOR SPOUSES

Family members of retired and disabled workers may be eligible to receive auxiliary benefits. But there is a ceiling on how much a family can receive on the earnings of a worker.

Spouse Benefits for Persons 60 and Over. Prior to 2000, older spouses of retired workers essentially receive the higher of either the benefit based on their earnings or a benefit equal to between 37.5 and 50 percent of the retired worker's PIA. If you are married and your spouse begins to receive benefits, then you are eligible at age 65 for a benefit equal to 50 percent of your spouse's PIA. By the way, common law marriages in states that acknowledge them often entitle both persons to the same benefits as any other married couple with the same coverage. Your spouse benefit is permanently reduced by 25/36 percent of PIA for each month of receipt before age 65. So, if you accept reduced spouse benefits at the earliest age, 62, your benefit would be 37.5 percent of your husband's or wife's PIA. As later normal retirement ages are phased in, beginning in 2000, the benefit amount for early acceptance of spouse benefits will be somewhat smaller, with ultimately a minimum value of 32.5 percent.

Would a spouse benefit be any different if the worker, instead of waiting to retire at 65, began receiving reduced early retirement benefits at an earlier age? No. The only way it is reduced is if the spouse collects it before age 65. Let's say a worker decides not to collect benefits at 65. Can the spouse receive benefits? Generally not. With the exception of certain divorced spouses, the worker must receive retirement benefits for a spouse to be eligible for spouse benefits. It's important to know also that spouses are eligible for Medicare at age 65 if their spouses are 62 or older.

Spouse Benefits for Fathers and Mothers With a Child Under 16 or a Disabled Child 16 or Over. Regardless of age, the spouse of a retired worker who is caring for a child under 16 or regularly performing personal services for a child of any age who was disabled before age 22 is eligible for a spouse benefit equal to 50 percent of the retired worker's PIA. Mother or father spouse benefits used to be continued until the youngest child (nondisabled) reached 18, but the age is now 16.

Benefits for Divorced Spouses. Can divorced spouses receive spouse benefits based on the earnings histories of their former spouses? Yes, under certain circumstances. A spouse who had been married to an eligible retired worker at least 10 years before their divorce is eligible for spouse benefits equal to 50 percent of the PIA if caring for a dependent child under age 16 or a disabled adult child as described above. Currently, divorced spouses who had been married for ten years are also eligible for benefits ranging from 37.5 percent of the PIA at age 62 to 50 percent at age 65, and for Medicare at age 65.

The 1983 amendments made a change in the eligibility requirements, which allow, beginning in 1985, a divorced spouse age 62 or over who has been divorced for two or more years to receive divorced spouse benefits regardless of whether the former spouse receives benefits (as long as the former spouse is fully insured and at least age 62).

BENEFITS FOR YOUR CHILDREN

Under certain circumstances, the children of retired or disabled workers are eligible to receive benefits, as are surviving children. These benefits are also generally available to legally adopted children, stepchildren, and children born out of wedlock who have acquired the right to inherit property from the covered worker or have been acknowledged in writing by the biological father. A financially dependent grandchild (or stepgrandchild) living with a retired grandparent (or great-grandparent) may also be eligible for benefits if natural or adoptive parents are deceased or disabled. The size of these benefits is subject to the family maximum.

Children's and Grandchildren's Benefits. Unmarried dependent children and grandchildren under age 18 may be eligible for a benefit equal to 50 percent of the retired or disabled worker's PIA. Also, unmarried dependent children and grandchildren age 18 (and in some cases until 2 months after reaching age 19) who are full-time elementary or secondary students may receive such benefits. However, the college student benefits which were formerly available under Social Security were, unfortunately, eliminated.

Disabled Child's Benefit. The same benefits, 50 percent of the PIA, may be payable in certain cases to the unmarried disabled children of retired or disabled workers regardless of age, if the disability began before age 22. Does this mean that a 25-year old disabled child is definitely not eligible for these benefits, if he or she has not applied? No, if the disabled child can prove the disabling condition began before age 22, then eligibility can still be established. Disabled children also receive Medicare benefits after 24 months on the benefit rolls.

WHAT IS THE FAMILY MAXIMUM?

The family maximum places a ceiling on the amount of monthly benefits that can be paid on a worker's earnings record. Otherwise, large families might receive much larger benefits than smaller ones with similar earnings histories. A formula applied to the worker's PIA yields a family maximum ranging from 150 to 188 percent of the PIA, depending on the worker's PIA. In disability cases since 1980, the family maximum is always smaller—85 percent of the AIME or 150 percent of the PIA, whichever is smaller—but not less than 100 percent of the PIA.

When the family maximum is exceeded, the benefit payable to a retired or disabled worker is not reduced. However, all other benefits payable on that worker's earnings record *are* proportionately reduced. One important exception to this rule affects divorced spouses who receive benefits based on a retired or disabled worker's earnings record; those benefits will not affect the family maximum level of other persons eligible for auxiliary benefits. The same is true for surviving divorced spouses (unless they are receiving benefits as a parent of an eligible child).

REDUCTIONS FOR NON-COVERED EMPLOYMENT

Your Social Security benefit *may* be smaller than you anticipated if you receive a public-employee pension from work not covered by Social Security *and* are also eligible to receive spouse or surviving spouse benefits under Social Security. Because of the government pension offset, your Social Security benefit *may* be reduced by two dollars for every three you receive from your government pension.

Also, your Social Security benefit (and that of your spouse and dependents) may be smaller than anticipated if you are first eligible after 1985 for *both* a Social Security benefit based on your own earnings record *and* a pension from non-covered public or private employment. For some persons in this circumstance, a different benefit formula may be used to compute their benefits, resulting in smaller benefits. This alternative formula and the government pension offset are both designed to reduce an unintended windfall for some people who also have pensions from non-covered employment.

Remember, not everyone in these circumstances is affected. If you think these provisions of the law might apply to you, contact Social Security and ask for further explanation.

GOING OUT OF THE COUNTRY?

If you're receiving monthly benefits and planning to be out of the country for an extended period of time (a period of 30 days or more), contact your local Social Security office to find out whether checks can be sent, for how long, and to make necessary arrangements to receive them. Checks can usually be sent for at least six months and often longer. However, there are a few countries (for example, East Germany) where checks cannot be sent.

BENEFITS UNDER
TWO EARNINGS RECORDS

Sometimes a person is entitled to benefits under two earnings records. For instance, a person may be entitled to a benefit as a retired worker on his or her own earnings record or as a spouse on his or her wife's or husband's record. When this happens a person essentially receives the benefit that results in a higher monthly payment, unless it is ultimately to his or her advantage to do otherwise. A special family maximum can also apply in these situations.

HOW DOES THE EARNINGS TEST WORK?

There are two earnings limits—one for nondisabled beneficiaries aged below 65 ($6000 in 1987) and one for people age 65 through 69 ($8160 in 1987). If you are age 70 or older you can earn as much as you want, and it will not affect your benefits. But if you're a retired worker, spouse, widow, widower, or dependent child beneficiary you will lose one dollar for every two dollars of earnings in excess of the earnings ceiling.

Under this formula, you really have to earn a considerable amount of money before you would lose all your benefits. For example, let's say you're 65 and receive a monthly retirement benefit of $500—that's $6000 a year in Social Security payments. Here's how the earnings test would affect you at different levels of earnings:

EFFECT OF EARNINGS TEST ON A RETIRED BENEFICIARY ENTITLED TO A $6000 YEARLY SOCIAL SECURITY BENEFIT IN 1987

	CASE 1	CASE 2	CASE 3	CASE 4
Amount of Earnings	$ 8,000	$10,000	$14,000	$20,160
Social Security Benefit	$ 6,000	$ 5,080	$ 3,080	0
Reduction in Social Security Benefit	0	$ 920	$ 2,920	$ 6,000
Total Income	$14,000	$15,080	$17,080	$20,160

In the example, you would lose your entire retirement benefit only if you earned $20,160 or more. You would, however, receive delayed retirement credits. Also your Medicare eligibility would not be affected.

The earnings of a retired worker can reduce other benefits based on that worker's earnings records. If someone collecting benefits on your earnings record earns in excess of the earnings ceiling, their benefit will be reduced or stopped, but their earnings will not affect anyone else receiving benefits on your earnings record.

There are some tricky aspects to the earnings test. First, you need to estimate in advance how much you expect to earn in a year and let Social Security know. Corrections are made later if you've undershot or overshot. Second, there's a special monthly rule that can apply, if it's to your advantage, in the year you retire. During that year, the earnings limit on regularly employed persons is calculated on a monthly basis—allowing you to earn one-twelfth the annual limit each month ($680 a month if you retired at age 65 to 69 in 1987, $500 if you're under 65). Under this special monthly rule, self-employed persons can generally receive benefits in the first year as long as they do not perform substantial services, defined in all cases as self-employment not over 15 hours a month and usually defined as 45 hours or less. Third, beginning the first full year you are receiving retirement benefits, you can earn up to the annual ceiling at any time during the year.

The 1983 amendments contained an additional liberalization of the earnings test. Beginning in 1990, benefits will be reduced by one dollar for every *three* dollars in excess of the earnings ceiling, for persons who reach full retirement age (65 in 1990).

COST-OF-LIVING ADJUSTMENT

The COLA is one of the most valuable features of Social Security. Once benefits are received, it guarantees their purchasing power. The availability of this benefit is one of the reasons it's no longer true that the elderly are hurt more by inflation than just about any other group.

Survivor's Benefits

None of us wants to die, but we all know there's more than a good chance that one day we will. Therefore we try, as best we can, to protect our loved ones from the financial problems that could accompany our death.

Not so long ago, children were sometimes separated from young widowed mothers simply for lack of financial support, and older widows risked ending up in county poorhouses. For example, in 1913 a New York State Commission found that 2716 children of 1483 widows were in state institutions only because their mothers could not afford their support. This horrible situation changed because of the widespread availability of Social Security as well as other forms of public and private protection against loss of income due to death of a worker.

Each month Social Security provides checks to nearly eight million survivor beneficiaries—young children, surviving widowed mothers and fathers, aged widows and widowers, and even, in some rare instances, to surviving parents.

BENEFITS FOR THE WIDOWED

Widow and Widower Benefits. Spouses aged 60 and over of fully insured workers are eligible for aged widow or widower's benefits upon the death of the worker.

The benefits range between 71.5 and 100 percent of the PIA. In fact, it can be higher if the deceased worker had earned delayed retirement credits. Aged widow or widower's benefits can be, and usually are, less than 100 percent of the PIA because of the following reasons:

- these benefits are subject to a rule that a survivor generally cannot get a higher benefit than the deceased worker would

be getting if living.* So, if the deceased worker had accepted reduced early retirement benefits, his or her spouse's widow or widower's benefit would also be permanently reduced;
- they are permanently reduced for each month of receipt before age 65 (by 19/40 of a percent of the PIA per month for persons reaching age 60 before 2000). So, for example, widow or widower's benefits at age 60 equals 71.5 percent of the deceased worker's PIA.

Widow or widower's benefits are also subject to the earnings test and family maximum. Also, accepting reduced widow's or widower's benefits from age 60 to 61 will result in reduction in a person's retirement or disability benefits if they become eligible for these benefits later, but taking a reduced widow or widower's benefits from 62 to 64 will have no such effect. Accepting reduced retirement benefits (or reduced spouse benefits) will have no bearing on the size of the widow's or widower's benefits a person may ultimately receive.

These benefit reductions are permanent. However, prior to age 65 a widow or widower may elect to discontinue receipt of reduced benefits to avoid further permanent benefit reduction.

A widow or widower's Social Security benefits may increase under certain circumstances. For instance, a widow who receives survivor's benefits at age 60 might, on her own earnings record, be eligible for a larger retirement benefit at age 62 or later. Or, she might remarry and be eligible, under her new husband's earning record, for either a larger aged-spouse benefit or, should her second husband die, an aged-widow's benefit.

Disabled Widow(er) Aged 50 to 59. Monthly benefits are payable to widows and widowers age 50 through 59 without dependent children only if they, themselves, are disabled, meeting disability requirements that are somewhat more strict than those applied to disabled workers. Beginning in January 1984, all disabled widow and widowers receive a benefit equal to 71.5 percent of the PIA. Before this change, benefits were reduced

---

* Under certain circumstances the aged widow(er)'s benefit is guaranteed to be at least 82.5 percent of the deceased worker's PIA.

for each month of receipt before age 60, to as little as 50 percent of the PIA at age 50. While generally helpful, this increase had some unexpected, negative consequences for a small group of low-income disabled widow(er)s, raising their incomes just enough so they were no longer eligible for SSI and, in turn, for Medicaid. A recent change in the law makes it possible to restore Medicaid eligibility for these people, but, *they must apply to their State Medicaid agency before July 1987.*

After a two-year waiting period, disabled widow(er)s are eligible to receive Medicare benefits as well. Even if someone is widowed between ages 60 and 63, it may make sense to apply for a special type of disabled widow or widower's status—disabled widow(er), Medicare only—so as to be eligible for benefits before 65. This will not affect the monthly benefit.

Surviving Mother's and Father's Benefits. A widow or widower of a worker who was fully or currently insured is eligible to receive surviving mother's or father's benefits at any age *if caring for a child under age 16 or a disabled child who is also eligible for survivor's benefits on the worker's record.* The monthly benefit is 75 percent of the deceased worker's PIA, although it is subject to both the family maximum and earnings test.

Can Surviving Divorced Spouses Receive Widow's or Widower's Benefits? Yes. Like the divorced spouses whose former marital partners are still living, divorced spouses are often eligible for survivors' benefits on the death of their former partners. The qualifications for benefits for divorced aged widows and widowers, disabled widows or widowers, and surviving mothers or fathers are essentially the same as for nondivorced survivors except that the marriage must have lasted for at least 10 years.

Will I lose Some or All of My Widow's or Widower's Benefits if I Remarry? Once, the answer to this question was always yes. You remember, there was much outrage, particularly over the plight of older widows, who, if they fell in love and remarried, lost a substantial portion of their benefits.

However, the law was changed in 1977 to allow surviving spouses aged 60 and over to keep their benefits if they remarry.

Further, the 1983 amendments corrected a technical error that did not give surviving divorced spouses this same right, and also extended this option to disabled widow(er)s aged 50 to 59.

What happens if you're a surviving mother or father who remarries? If you are under 60, you lose your benefits. The same is true for a divorced surviving mother or father. If this new marriage ends, you may again be eligible for benefits. Will your children's benefits be reduced if you remarry? No, and they might even increase. If your family benefits had been reduced because of the family maximum, then the benefits children get will be larger because *you* will no longer receive benefits.

Other Recent Changes in Widow's and Widower's Benefits. The 1983 amendments provided a new way for calculating initial benefit amounts for widows and widowers who become eligible for benefits after 1984 and whose spouses had died before reaching age 62. Beginning in 1985, the earnings record of a worker who had died many years ago is updated just the way that of a retired worker is—by changes in average wages if that produces a larger benefit. This means that for people widowed at an early age, aged widow's and widower's benefits are generally larger—and never less—than they would have been.

For persons born in or after 1940, the retirement age changes included in the 1983 amendments also affect the age of eligibility for full widow's or widower's benefits and slightly reduces the benefit for persons accepting widow(er)'s benefits between ages 60 and the age of eligibility for full benefits. The largest reductions will occur for persons born in 1962 or later.

SURVIVING CHILDREN'S BENEFITS

Surviving children under age 18, surviving children of any age who were disabled before age 22, and surviving children ages 18 and, in some cases, 19 who are full-time elementary or secondary school students are eligible for monthly benefits if a parent, or in some cases, grandparent, was fully or currently insured at the time of death. The rules governing receipt of surviving children's benefits are essentially the same as the rules governing eligibility for dependent children's benefits on the earnings record of a retired or disabled worker (see Chapter 8). Surviving children receive a benefit equal to 75 percent of the PIA of the deceased worker subject, of course, to the family maximum and the earnings test.

SURVIVING PARENT'S BENEFITS

Under certain circumstances the dependent parent aged 62 or over of a fully insured deceased worker is also eligible for a survivor's benefit. The deceased worker must have provided at least half the financial support of the parent. Parents are defined as biological parents, parents who adopted the deceased worker before age 16 and stepparents caring for the deceased worker before that worker was 16.

The parent's benefit equals 82.5 percent of the PIA where only one parent receives the benefit and 75 percent each when both are beneficiaries, subject to the family maximum.

LUMP-SUM DEATH PAYMENT

A lump-sum death payment of $255 is generally made to the surviving spouse who was living with a deceased worker. Divorced spouses are not eligible. In certain cases, where no surviving spouse is present, the benefit is paid only if there are children eligible for monthly survivor's checks in the month of the death of the worker. Application for the lump-sum death payment should be made within two years of the worker's death. Everyone must apply to receive it, except widow(er)s who were living with the deceased worker at the time of death and were receiving a spouse benefit before the worker's death. They automatically receive this payment without applying.

IF YOU BECOME DISABLED

Social Security protects against loss of income because of long-term disability, but you must be severely disabled to qualify. Low-income workers applying for disability benefits through the Supplement Security Income (SSI) program also have to meet this definition of disability. Despite the strict eligibility criteria, no public or private program provides greater protection to Americans against the risk of disability.

During a typical month in 1986, the Disability Insurance (DI) program paid benefits to approximately 2.7 million disabled workers and 1.3 million family members, totaling about $20 billion during the year. Benefits were also paid each month to more than 100,000 disabled widows and widowers and over 540,000 adult children disabled before age 22. Despite the strict eligibility criteria, no public or private program provides greater protection to Americans against the risk of disability. Also, each month about 2.7 million persons received disability benefits through SSI—sharing about $8 billion in payments to blind and disabled persons during the year.

People who are so disabled that they qualify for Social Security or SSI disability programs need them. Those who suggest that large numbers of disability beneficiaries are malingerers are simply being unfair. This is why recent administrative procedures resulting in the removal of several hundred thousand beneficiaries, especially the mentally impaired, stirred so much controversy and public outrage.

DISABILITY BENEFITS

If you become disabled, after a five-month waiting period you are eligible to receive monthly benefits equal to 100 percent of your PIA for the duration of your period of disability. At the normal retirement age (currently age 65), your disability benefits will automatically become retirement benefits.

What about your family? If you have children under age 18 (older in some cases), a child age 18 or older who became disabled before age 22, a spouse (or divorced former spouse) who's caring for a child under 16 or your disabled child, or a spouse age 62 or over, then they, too, are probably eligible to receive monthly benefits. Benefits for family members of disabled workers are identical to those for retired workers except that the family maximum is lower. (See Chapter 8 for more details.)

After what amounts to a 29-month waiting period (the five-month waiting period plus the first 24 months of entitlement to disability benefits), disabled workers, disabled widow and widowers age 50 through 64, and adult disabled children age 18 or over who were disabled before age 22 are eligible for all Medicare benefits. Medicare does not, however, cover the other family members of disabled workers (except for a spouse who is 65 or over).

A disabled worker can be entitled retroactively to both cash benefits and Medicare benefits. There's a five-month waiting period before a disabled worker can receive cash benefits. If the onset of your disability occurred before the date of your application, however, you may have a right to retroactive benefits—perhaps, under unusual circumstances, to as much as 12 months' worth. As for Medicare, under unusual circumstances you can receive up to 12 months' retroactive eligibility, which means you have to wait only 12 months after your date of application for Medicare benefits to begin.

WORKER'S AGE AT DISABILITY	NUMBER OF DROP-OUT YEARS
Under 27	0
27-31	1
32-36	2
37-41	3
42-46	4
47 and over	5

You can appeal a favorable decision entitling you to disability benefits. Why do that? You might appeal if the discussion allows you to receive monthly disability benefits beginning five months after you applied for them, if you believe you were actually disabled many months before you applied for benefits. If you win the appeal, you might receive retroactive benefits.

HOW ARE BENEFITS CALCULATED?

Benefits are calculated for disabled workers in nearly the same way as for retirees. A major difference is that the years counted to determine earnings and the number of quarters required include only those until the year that Social Security determines the disability began, rather than until age 62. In another major difference, retired workers, and disabled workers age 47 and over, drop out the five lowest years of earnings from calculation of their average indexed monthly earnings (AIME). Generally, the more drop-out years you have, the higher your benefit. Disabled workers under 47 have fewer drop-out years.

In certain cases, young disabled workers might also be able to drop out up to two years for years in which they were caring for a child under three and had no earnings. But in such cases, their total number of drop-out years cannot be more than three.

Before the Social Security Disability Amendments of 1980, all disabled workers were allowed five drop-out years. Why the change? It was argued that allowing the same number of drop-out years for younger workers gave them considerable advantage over older disabled workers who had to use more years of low earnings when calculating their average indexed monthly earnings. Others have pointed out, though, that older disabled workers may now have an advantage because they had a better chance to reach their full earnings capacity.

There's a "disability freeze" that protects you and your family against reductions in your other Social Security benefits because you are unable to earn income while disabled. The length of time you are disabled does not count against you in determining your insured status or size of benefit.

Disability benefits are subject to a more restrictive maximum family benefit. Responding to the concern that large benefits for some workers and their families might encourage some persons to apply for disability benefits and discourage some beneficiaries from returning to work, the 1980 Disability Amendments reduced the maximum amount of benefits that newly disabled workers and their families can receive. The new maximum family benefit equals the lesser of 85 percent of the AIME or 150 percent of the Primary Insurance Amount, but in all cases must be at least 100 percent of the PIA. But because disabled workers often have childrearing expenses, personal care expenses, less savings than retired workers, and often have not reached peak earnings potential when disabled, this new family maximum may be too restrictive.

Under certain circumstances, Social Security disability benefits are reduced for workers and their families if they are also receiving Workers' Compensation benefits or some types of disability benefits payable under certain federal, state, or local programs. Receipt of veteran's benefits, needs-tested benefits, private pension, and private insurance benefits will not affect your disability benefits.

To qualify for disability benefits, a worker must meet the insured status requirements (see Chapter 7 for definitions) and be severely disabled as defined under the law. A disabled worker must be both fully insured and disability insured, except for those disabled by blindness who only need to meet the fully insured requirement.

HOW IS DISABILITY DEFINED?

To be eligible for disability benefits under either the Social Security Disability Insurance program or the Supplemental Security Income (SSI) program, you must meet the same very strict definition of disability. You must be unable to engage in any substantial gainful activity by reason of any medically determinable physical or mental impairment which can be expected to result in death or which has lasted or can be expected to last at least 12 months. Taking into consideration age, education, and previous work experience, a worker must be unable to do any kind of work that exists in the national economy. In other words, the availability of jobs is not taken into consideration.

This definition of disability also applies to a disabled child's benefit. Believe it or not, the disability criteria for a disabled widow or widower are even stricter, because age, education, and work experience are not taken into account.

For most disabled workers, substantial gainful activity (SGA), sometimes called substantial gainful work is defined as the ability to earn more than a limited amount a month from employment—$300 in 1986 ($650 for blind people). You don't have to *earn* this amount to be ineligible for benefits; you just need to be *able* to earn it. Although the dollar amount that defines substantial gainful activity may be revised periodically by the Department of Health and Human Services, there has been no revision since 1980. For blind persons, the test is more lenient. Blindness is defined as 20/200 or less vision in the better eye with the use of corrective lenses or a visual field reduction to 20 degrees or less.

When deciding whether someone is engaged in substantial gainful activity, Social Security deducts from earnings the cost of certain impairment-related items and services that an individual must pay in order to work (e.g. prostheses, attendant care services). The amount of any subsidy from work performed under special conditions (e.g. sheltered workshop) is also deducted.

WHAT HAPPENS IF I APPLY?

The local Social Security office first takes your application, including the names of physicians and medical institutions that have treated you, a description of your disability, and information about your work experience (and, for SSI disability applications, information about your income and assets). Your application can be turned down at this level if you do not meet the insured status requirement or if you are (or are capable of) engaging in substantial gainful activity. (Your SSI application can be turned down at this level if you have excess income or resources).

If your application gets through this first step, it's forwarded to the state agency that makes disability determinations, called the state disability determination service (DDS). They decide whether you have a severe impairment that significantly limits your physical or mental capacity to work. No account is taken of your age, work experience, or education.

If you have a severe impairment, your state DDS decides whether your impairment meets or equals the standards specified in the list of impairments developed by Social Security and whether it is expected to last (or has lasted) at least one year. If it does, you're eligible. If the impairment doesn't meet the standards, but is expected to last (or has lasted) one year, then you might still be eligible.

A decision is made then about your ability to perform past work. If you can, you are not eligible. If you cannot, then vocational factors (age, work experience, and education) are taken into account to determine whether your disability prevents you from performing *other* work that exists in the national economy. This becomes very important at ages 50 and over, because the vocational factors are designed, in part, to compensate for the increased difficulty in performing substantial gainful work with advancing age.

The Reagan administration 1981 proposals to eliminate nonmedical factors from the disability determination process met with much protest. Many believed this specific change would leave many disabled older workers without benefits and with little likelihood of being able to work. In fact, many Social Security experts have recommended that the determination of disability at older ages should be eased, not made stricter.

WHAT IS VOCATIONAL REHABILITATION?

Let's say you're awarded disability benefits. It's possible that you will be offered vocational rehabilitation services such as training, counseling, medical services, or job placement. If offered, you must accept them for your benefits to continue. If not offered, you might want to contact your state vocational rehabilitation agency anyway to see what services they can provide you. Receiving vocational rehabilitation services will not affect your checks unless your disability improves or you perform substantial gainful activity.

DON'T FORGET YOUR RIGHT TO APPEAL

If your application for disability benefits has been rejected (or if you have been terminated after a periodic review) and you believe that you are unable to work because of your disability, you should appeal within 60 days of receiving notice from Social Security. Remember: It's your right and there's a high rate of reversal of initial rejections (see Chapter 6).

PERIODIC REVIEWS: WHAT TO EXPECT

Depending on the nature of your disability, your eligibility will be reviewed : (1) within six to 18 months if medical improvement is anticipated; (2) every three years if medical improvement is possible; or (3) every five to seven years if improvement is not anticipated. SSI recipients are also subject to review (generally yearly) to make sure they still meet the administrative criteria for eligibility, mainly the income and assets tests.

Although the periodic reviews, mandated by the 1980 Disability amendments, have been highly controversial, more recent changes in the law and administrative reforms have improved the review process (see Chapter 5). SSA reports that now "disability payments generally will continue unless there is substantial proof of both *medical* improvement *and ability* to work." Also, the combined effects of multiple non-severe impairments are now taken into consideration. Further, if a decision that you are no longer disabled is rendered by the state disability agency, you have a right to request, within 60 days of receiving notice, a face-to-face interview with a hearing officer to state your case. Such an interview may result in a recommendation of continued eligibility. After that, you may appeal to the administrative law judge, Appeals Council, and federal court. It is possible to continue to receive benefits through June 1988 while appealing a decision through the Administrative Law Judge level (see Chapter 6), but you must file your appeal and request continuation of benefits within 10 days of receiving notice of initial denial of benefits, and then again if you if you receive notice of denial of benefits at the reconsideration level of appeal. You should know that you may have to pay back some or all of your benefits if you lose all your appeals and if SSA does not grant a waiver of the overpayment.

WHAT IF YOU RETURN TO WORK

Benefits stop if a beneficiary recovers medically from the disabling condition and is able to work or becomes able to perform substantial gainful activity. In the past, disability insurance beneficiaries were often reluctant to try working because they risked losing monthly benefits and Medicare benefits. (SSI beneficiaries faced similar problems.) The 1980 Disability Amendments included several provisions designed to strengthen work incentives:

- automatic reentitlement to DI and SSI benefits for up to 15 months after completing a 9-month trial work period (assuming no medical recovery has occurred);
- continued Medicare benefits, generally for three years after DI benefits cease because of return to work;
- waiver of the next 24-month waiting period for Medicare benefits, or credit for the number of months already earned toward the waiting period if a worker begins receiving disability benefits within five years after they ended or a disabled widow or widower or adult disabled child begins receiving benefits within seven years;
- extension of the opportunity for a trial work period to disabled widows or widowers. (Previously, only disabled workers and disabled adult children were eligible for the trial work period);

- exclusion of impairment-related work expenses when determining substantial gainful activity.

WHAT'S THE TRIAL WORK PERIOD?

DI beneficiaries can have up to nine months to test their ability to work without any loss of benefits. Generally, months of earnings of $75 or more count as trial months. If the beneficiary is able to engage in substantial gainful activity (or if medical recovery occurs during the trial work period), at the end of the nine-month period (not necessarily consecutive months), then three months of adjustment benefits are provided for the worker. Medicare benefits can continue for three years after these cash benefits end.

THE DETERMINATION IS COMPLEX

Making disability determinations is very difficult. Besides rejecting applications that should be accepted, it's also possible to do the reverse or for people to recover just enough to be no longer eligible, though this is probably less common under current standards. The periodic reviews and reporting procedures are designed to weed out the relatively few recipients who really are ineligible. There's nothing wrong with that. The reason so much criticism was directed at the Continuing Disability Reviews is that they seemed to be removing far too many people who were truly disabled.

As things stand now, given the strictness of our disability definition, we probably have many more errors resulting from improperly excluding disabled people from benefits than errors of inclusion.

MEDICARE BENEFITS

The Medicare program was established in 1965 in response to great concern about the high, sometimes prohibitively high, cost of medical care of older Americans. Since then this program has grown so that during a typical month in 1987, almost the entire aged population, about 28 million persons, as well as 3 million disabled persons and 100,000 persons with end-stage renal disease, are partially protected against the high cost of medical care. Program costs will be about at $85 billion in 1987, with Medicare payments averaging about $2450 per aged and $3200 per disabled beneficiary.

MEDICARE AND MEDICAID: THE DIFFERENCE

Is Medicare the same as Medicaid? No. The right to benefits through Medicare is established primarily by payroll tax contributions. Under Medicaid, the right is established by financial need. Medicare provides benefits to the aged (65 and over), blind, disabled, and persons with permanent kidney failure. In general, Medicaid, which is paid out of federal, state, and local revenues, provides benefits to aged, blind and disabled SSI recipients, families receiving benefits through Aid to Families with Dependent Children, and certain medically needy persons. Medicare's benefits are mainly for treatment of acute illness, primarily in hospital settings. Medicaid funds this type of care, but it also provides benefits for chronic health care problems, primarily in nursing homes. Neither program provides much support for the treatment of chronic illness in the home (sometimes called "community care" or "homecare"). (See Chapter 12 for information about Medicaid.)

SOME OF MEDICARE'S SHORTCOMINGS

Although it has done much to increase access to health care for the aged and disabled and to improve the quality of life for all Americans, Medicare is not without its problems. It is costly; an estimated $54 billion will be spent in 1987 through its Hospital Insurance (HI) program and $31 billion through its Supplementary Medical Insurance (SMI). Rising health care costs, the need for medical services among a growing aged population, and a general lack of cost controls across the entire health care system will—barring remedial legislation—result in the depletion of the HI Trust Fund, most probably in the mid-to-late 1990's. Of course, it's better than a good bet that Congress will act to remedy, if not resolve, this problem before then.

Medicare benefits sometimes do not match the needs of the aged and disabled. Many do not realize until it is too late that *Medicare provides extremely limited protection against the cost of long-term care* resulting from chronic illness. It focuses, instead, on acute illness—illness requiring immediate, but not prolonged, treatment. Little emphasis is placed on prevention.

Medicare does not fully protect against the high cost of health care. No catastrophic health care protection is provided. Though less likely under Medicare, it is still possible to lose your entire savings by paying for health care services. More importantly, Medicare covers slightly less than one-half (45 percent for the aged) of the total health care bill of aged and disabled beneficiaries. Other public programs (see Chapter 12), primarily the means-tested Medicaid program, provide additional protection. But much of the remaining cost comes directly from the beneficiaries' pockets. In fact, a recent House Aging Committee study estimated that the elderly spent an average of about $1850 per person of their own resources—16 percent of their income—on health care in 1986.

Despite problems, Medicare does increase the economic security and access to health care for millions of Americans. Without Medicare, most of the aged or disabled would find the cost of comparable health insurance extremely high, and many simply could not afford adequate health care. Many younger family members would have to choose between paying for the health care needed by their elders or allowing their elderly relatives to go without adequate health care.

WHO IS ELIGIBLE FOR MEDICARE BENEFITS?

Almost everyone age 65 and over, as well as many disabled, are eligible for Medicare Part A, Hospital Insurance (HI), and Medicare Part B, Supplementary Medical Insurance (SMI) benefits. HI covers most hospital-based services, follow-up care in a skilled nursing facility, hospice care, and limited home care services. You are eligible for benefits:

- if you are 65 or over and qualify for Social Security or Railroad Retirement monthly cash benefits. (Remember you do not actually have to receive monthly benefits, just be eligible to receive them);
- after you have been entitled for 24 months to Social Security as a disabled worker, disabled widow(er), child age 18 or over who was disabled before age 22, or under certain circumstances if you receive Railroad Retirement disability benefits;
- if you have permanent kidney failure and require dialysis or a kidney transplant. (You may qualify on the basis of kidney failure if you receive a monthly Social Security or Railroad Retirement benefit, if you are currently or fully insured, or the spouse, widow(er) or dependent child of such a person);
- under special provisions if you were born before 1909 and have few or no quarters of coverage.

In 1983, all federal employees began making payroll contributions into the HI Trust Fund. Credit toward Medicare eligibility for most workers and their families has been given for past federal employment that was not subject to the payroll tax.

If you are 65 and over and do not qualify for HI benefits under any of the above criteria, you may purchase this protection by paying a monthly premium roughly equal to the insurance value of the benefit, $226 per month through 1987 (premiums change each January 1). You must enroll between January 1 and March 31. Your premium may be 10 percent higher if there was a period of at least one year in which you could have had HI but were not enrolled. This increase only applies to twice the number of years for which you were late in enrolling.

What about eligibility for Medicare Part B, the Supplementary Medical Insurance Program (SMI) program, which pays for physician services, certain outpatient services, limited home health services and certain health services and supplies?

- people entitled to HI benefits are eligible to enroll in this voluntary program, which requires payment of a monthly premium—$17.90 in 1987;
- people 65 and over who are U.S. citizens or lawfully admitted aliens with five continuous years of residence may enroll even though they are not eligible for HI benefits.

HOW TO ENROLL FOR MEDICARE

Although Medicare is administered by the Health Care Financing Administration, your local Social Security office handles applications for Medicare, provides information, and helps you file claims.

HI enrollment is automatic at age 65 for those already receiving monthly Social Security or Railroad Retirement checks before age 65. Otherwise, you should apply for HI benefits about three months before your 65th birthday. If you are over 65 and not receiving HI protection, it's not too late to enroll. Just call your local Social Security office. In case you delayed filing your application for Hospital Insurance until after your 65th birthday, benefits can be retroactive up to six months under HI, but not under SMI.

Disabled Social Security beneficiaries (disabled workers, disabled widow(er)s ages 50 through 64 and disabled children age 18 or over who were disabled before age 18) are also automatically enrolled in the HI program at the end of a 5-month waiting period and the first 24 months of entitlement to DI benefits. Under certain circumstances eligibility for Medicare benefits can begin as early as 12 to 23 months after initial receipt of DI benefits, if the onset of the disability is determined as having occurred before filing the DI application. A special status called "Disabled Widow(er)s Medicare Only" allows some widows and widowers aged 60 through 64 not collecting disability benefits to qualify for Medicare. You might qualify even if you are collecting surviving spouse, mother's, or father's benefits. Also, disabled federal workers might be eligible to enroll in HI after the first 24 months of eligibility for DI benefits.

How do you get SMI? It's usually very simple. You will be automatically enrolled (unless you are a resident of Puerto Rico or a foreign country) when your HI protection begins. In most cases, the monthly SMI premium, $17.90 in 1987, is deducted from monthly Social Security checks. The premium is now set through 1988 at a level equal to 25 percent of the SMI program costs for the aged, with the federal treasury (general revenues) paying the rest.

If you don't want Medicare SMI protection, you must tell Social Security that you decline it when you apply or otherwise become eligible for HI protection.

Certain people must apply for SMI protection, including: those expecting to work past their 65th birthday; those who are 65 but ineligible for Hospital Insurance; people with permanent kidney failure; disabled widows and widowers age 60 to 64 not receiving disability checks; those eligible for Medicare because of federal employment; and those residing in Puerto Rico or in a foreign country. The initial enrollment period begins three months before the month you first become eligible for SMI and ends three months after that month. The first month of eligibility is usually the month you turn 65 or the 25th month of disability. Apply through your local Social Security office.

What if you do not sign up for SMI protection during the initial enrollment period, but later decide you want it? A general enrollment period exists during the first three months of each year. There may be a 10 percent increase in premiums for each 12-month period you delayed claiming these benefits.

Once enrolled, you may drop SMI coverage if you wish. Coverage can end also if you fail to pay your premium within a grace period (usually 90 days), if your disability benefit ends because you have recovered, 36 months after your disability ends if you are still disabled but able to participate in substantial gainful activity, or if you are receiving benefits as a result of the earnings record of your marital partner and you are divorced before 10 years of marriage.

Persons with end-stage renal disease are generally eligible to receive benefits about three months after the month during which maintenance dialysis treatment begins. Sometimes benefits can begin as early as the first month of end-stage renal disease for persons in a self-dialysis training program or for persons receiving a kidney transplant.

Is SMI a good buy? For nearly all it is because of a federal subsidy worth approximately three times your premium.

Should you drop private insurance when you become eligible for Medicare? Be extremely careful in making any private health insurance decision. Be certain you know what you are giving up. It's often difficult for aged and disabled persons to pick up new protection later at affordable prices.

Should you purchase a "Medigap" policy, a private policy that picks up some of the costs Medicare does not cover? It may be a good idea but, again, you should proceed *very cautiously* before signing an insurance contract. Also, you should know that *"Medigap" policies do not provide significant protection against the cost of long term care* in nursing homes or community settings. For more information, you may want to call your Social Security office for a pamphlet entitled *Guide to Health Insurance for People with Medicare.*

If you or your spouse are working and have employer-based health insurance, recent changes in the law may apply to you.

For disabled beneficiaries and for persons 65 and over covered both under Medicare *and* employment-based health insurance, Medicare is now the secondary, rather than the primary, payer of health bills (unless you decide to cancel your employer-based health insurance). Another change allows such people to postpone enrollment in the SMI program, generally without being subject to late enrollment premium increases.

MEDICARE PART A (HI) BENEFITS

With Medicare's HI protection, you may receive benefits for: inpatient hospital care; care in a skilled nursing facility; home health care; and hospice care.

Inpatient Care in a Participating Hospital. The great bulk of Medicare expenditures go to pay for hospital costs for aged and disabled beneficiaries. To be eligible for reimbursement for hospital costs, you must need hospital care, have it prescribed by a physician, and be treated in a hospital that participates in

SERVICES COVERED AND NOT COVERED BY YOUR MEDICARE HOSPITAL INSURANCE (PART A)

IF YOU ARE A PATIENT IN A PARTICIPATING HOSPITAL OR SKILLED NURSING FACILITY

COVERED	
Semi-private room	Drugs provided by the hospital or skilled nursing facility
Meals, including special diets	Blood costs (ex. first 3 pints)
Regular nursing services	
Special care units in hospital (e.g., Intensive Care)	*NOT COVERED*
Operating and recovery room costs in hospital	Extra charges for a private room unless medically necessary
X rays, Lab tests, radiation therapy	Television, radio, telephone, laundry service, or other special convenience items or services
Medical supplies and use of appliances (casts, surgical dressings, wheelchair)	Private nursing
Rehabilitation Services (including speech, occupational, and physical therapy)	Doctor's charges (covered under Supplemental Medical Insurance)

Medicare. Almost all do, but you should check.

Up to 90 days of inpatient care for problems other than mental health are covered for each "spell of illness" or "benefit period." A new spell of illness begins, under Medicare's definition, on the first day you receive inpatient hospital care or certain types of care in a skilled nursing facility. It ends after 60 consecutive days in which you do not receive such care.

You must pay a deductible and make certain copayments during each benefit period. The deductibles and all copayments are generally increased each year at the same rate as payments to hospitals are adjusted for changes in hospital costs.

What's a deductible? It's the initial cost for care that you have to pay under the terms of Medicare's HI program. What's a copayment? It's a dollar amount that you must pay in addition to what HI pays. (It's similar to "coinsurance" which is the percentage of the cost of services that you pay under SMI).

In each benefit period (spell of illness), Medicare provides payment for covered inpatient hospital expenses:

- for the first 60 days of hospitalization for medical problems, after your deductible ($520 in 1987);
- for the 61st day through the 90th day, for which you copay ($130 per day in 1987).

If you ever require more than 90 days of inpatient hospital care during a benefit period, then Medicare provides you with a nonrenewable lifetime reserve. The lifetime reserve provides payment for covered hospital expenses:

- for up to an additional 60 days with you making a copayment ($260 per day in 1987). (Remember, once you use all 60 days, you no longer have a reserve and Medicare pays nothing for inpatient hospital care for the remainder of this benefit period. *Also note*: if you go through your 90 days in a benefit period, the hospital will begin using your lifetime reserve days unless you notify them in writing not to do so).

What about hospitalization for psychiatric care? The benefits, deductible, and copayments are the same, except that there is a 190-day lifetime limit on reimbursement for inpatient care in psychiatric hospitals. The limit may *not* apply to psychiatric services given in conjunction with inpatient treatments for medical illness and diagnosis.

Inpatient Care in a Participating Skilled Nursing Facility. After a hospital stay of at least 3 days, you may be eligible for rehabilitation and other health services if your doctor certifies that you need extended care in a skilled nursing facility. You must need these services on a daily basis for a condition for which you were treated in the hospital, and must be admitted to the skilled nursing facility within 30 days of leaving the hospital.

In each benefit period, Medicare's HI provides payment for covered services in a skilled nursing facility:

- for all costs in the first 20 days;
- for the 21st through 100th day for which you copay ($65.00 in 1986);
- for nothing after the 100th day.

Home Health Care Benefits. If you are homebound and need part-time skilled nursing care, physical therapy, or speech therapy, you may be eligible for certain home health care services through a participating home health agency—including part-time skilled nursing care, physical therapy, speech therapy, medical supplies, part-time home health aides, occupational therapy, and medical social services. Your doctor must certify your need and set up a home health plan. You do *not* need to have been hospitalized prior to receipt of these services.

Medicare's home health services have been a good step toward enabling people to receive care at home, avoiding possibly costlier treatment in hospital or other institutional settings. The basis of eligibility is limited, however, and only a fairly narrow range of services is funded.

Hospice Care for Dying Persons. Tax legislation in 1982 established hospice care services for HI beneficiaries with a life expectancy of fewer than six months. Medicare beneficiaries may

Hospice Services For Terminally Ill Persons*

COVERED	
Nursing care	Medical Supplies (including drugs and use of appliances)
Physical, speech, or occupational therapy	Physician services
Medical social services	Drugs, including drugs for relief of pain
Homemaker-home health aide services	
Short-term inpatient care (no more than 5 consecutive days)	*NOT COVERED*
Respite care (no more than 5 consecutive days)	Election of hospice care requires giving up certain other Medicare benefits

*Regulations on coverage and reimbursement of hospice care are still being developed.

choose hospice care as an alternative to other Medicare benefits for as many as 210 days, if a physician certifies terminal illness. If a patient lives longer than the 210 days and wishes to continue the service, then the hospice agency is required by law to continue providing service. With the exception of outpatient drugs and inpatient respite care (care given to the patient so that the care-givers at home can get a slight "respite"), there are no deductibles or copayments. At most, these copayments represent 5 percent of the cost of the drugs or respite care. This important benefit provides many services often needed during the last months of a terminal illness (see Table). However, because there are only 279 Medicare-certified hospices nationwide, in some areas they are not really accessible.

Other Hospital Insurance Benefits. Care provided in a Christian Science sanatorium may be paid through HI. Also, beneficiaries covered under either Medicare Part A (HI) or Part B (SMI) may choose to have health services provided by a Health Maintenance Organization (HMO) or some other competitive medical plan in their area if it is certified for participation in Medicare. Some HMOs and other such plans contract to provide a range of services to enrolled members.

MEDICARE PART B (SMI) BENEFITS

If you are enrolled in the SMI program, you receive benefits for certain doctor's services; other medical and health services including outpatient hospital services; and home health care.

SMI will generally pay for 80 percent of approved charges for most covered services, after you have paid the SMI deductible in a calendar year (now the first $75 of approved charges). The deductible and coinsurance do not apply to certain services such as home health visits, and you are responsible under SMI (and HI as well) to pay for the first three pints of blood you use unless you have the blood replaced.

Just because Medicare's SMI program pays 80 percent of approved charges, it does not follow that you are only responsible for 20 percent of what you are billed for services. A Medicare beneficiary who has paid the SMI deductible may be responsible for 20 percent of approved charges plus the portion of the medical bill that is in excess of approved charges, as well as for services not covered by SMI such as most drugs.

Doctor's Services. SMI helps pay for many doctor's services you might need, in an office visit, as an outpatient or as an inpatient. But most routine services like a regular physical, regular eye examination, regular foot care, the filling of a cavity, or making dentures are not covered. Also, SMI helps pay for a second opinion if surgery is recommended. Eighty percent of approved charges (after payment of the initial yearly deductible) for physician fees, for diagnostic, medical treatment, or surgical services performed are generally covered. Coverage for outpatient treatment of mental health problems is extremely limited, with SMI paying no more than $250 a year.

Other Medical and Health Services Including Outpatient Hospital Services. SMI also generally helps pay for diagnostic tests, X-rays, radiation therapy, drugs that cannot be self-administered, home dialysis, speech and physical therapy, emergency room and outpatient clinic services, hospital laboratory tests, ambulance transportation under certain conditions, medically necessary equipment such as wheelchairs and oxygen, prosthetic de-

Medicare Services Covered And Not Covered By Your Supplemental Medical Insurance (Part B)

COVERED

Medical and surgical services including: anesthesia, oral surgery, nonroutine foot care, chiropractic treatment for subluxation of the spine, surgical fees, radiology and pathology fees
Diagnostic Tests and Procedures (including X-rays)
Transfusions
Drugs that cannot be self-administered
Pneumococcal vaccine, immunizations required because of injury or risk of infection, Hepatitis B vaccine for persons at high risk
Ambulance service (under certain conditions)
Home health services
Outpatient physical and speech therapy
Services of your doctor's nurse
Medical supplies and use of appliances including: artificial limbs and eyes, home dialysis services, optometrists' services for fitting corrective lenses after cataract surgery, casts, surgical dressings, prosthetic devices, wheel-chairs, canes, walkers
Outpatient radiation therapy
Outpatient mental health services (up to $250 per year)

NOT COVERED

Routine physical examinations and tests related to such examinations
Routine foot care (except for diabetics)
Routine eye and hearing examinations, dental care
Most cosmetic surgery
Most prescription and non-prescription drugs
Most immunizations

IF YOU NEED HOME HEALTH SERVICES (THESE SERVICES ARE AVAILABLE UNDER YOUR SMI PROTECTION—AS WELL AS UNDER HOSPITAL INSURANCE PROTECTION).

COVERED

Part-time skilled nursing care
Physical therapy
Speech therapy
If any of the above services is required, Medicare might also pay for:
   Occupational Therapy
   Part-time service of home health aides
   Medical social services
Medical supplies and equipment provided by the agency

NOT COVERED

Full-time nursing care at home
Most drugs
Meals delivered or prepared in your home
Homemaker services

---

vices including artificial limbs, braces, colostomy bags, and corrective lenses after cataract surgery. Again, routine exams and services including most immunizations are not covered.

Home Health Care Services. Under certain conditions, your SMI covers certain home health services and no coinsurance or deductible payments are required, except the 20% coinsurance for durable medical equipment. The benefits and criteria for payments under SMI are essentially the same under HI.

In some cases, Medicare can pay up to 100 percent of the cost of outpatient surgery performed in a Medicare-certified outpatient surgical center. And, Medicare can also help pay for some outpatient rehabilitation services.

BENEFITS FOR PERMANENT KIDNEY FAILURE

Medicare has made life-saving treatments available to nearly every American with permanent kidney failure. Medicare covers a large portion of the costs associated with kidney transplant (including the cost of care for a donor). It also covers much of the cost of artificial kidney treatments (dialysis) for those with permanent kidney failure—including dialysis treatment at home or at an approved dialysis facility. And people covered due to permanent kidney failure are also eligible for the other Medicare services. If you or a member of your family may require benefits because of end-stage renal disease, call or write your Social Security office for a pamphlet entitled *Medicare Coverage of Kidney Dialysis and Kidney Transplant Services.*

PROS: WHAT YOU NEED TO KNOW

Peer Review Organizations (PROs) are groups of health professionals who review the hospital treatment of Medicare patients. Originally intended to serve as checks against the rising cost of medical care, PROs increasingly are taking on the function of safe-guarding the quality of care. PROs now do pre-admission reviews of whether Medicare should pay for certain surgical procedures, and also make decisions about when Medicare should no longer be responsible to pay for a hospital stay.

As a hospital patient, you have certain rights, including the right to be notified 48 hours in advance of when Medicare will no longer be responsible to cover bills. *If you receive such a notice, you have the right to appeal this decision to the PRO, and, if you ask for a priority review, the PRO must give you a decision within three days.* If you lose the appeal, you will not be responsible to pay for the continued stay until noon on the day after receiving notice of the decision on your appeal. To appeal call your PRO immediately, then write so that your appeal is on record. You can also appeal other adverse decisions of the PRO, the hospital, or insurance intermediary to the PRO concerning admissions or covered services, regardless of whether it was a decision of the PRO, the hospital, or the insurance intermediary. Notification forms informing you of adverse actions should provide information on how to contact your PRO.

You should also know that there is a Medicare fraud and abuse hot line. If you think you are being billed for services not received or receiving services you do not need, call the Inspector General's toll-free hot line (1-800-368-5779 except in Maryland, where it is 1-800-638-3986). Or write to: HHS, OIG, Hot Line, P.O. Box 17303, Baltimore, MD 21203-7303.

HOW HI PAYS YOUR MEDICAL BILLS

Reimbursement for your medical costs under the HI program is generally quite simple because the institution that treated you and the HI intermediary handle all the paperwork.

When you receive services covered under HI from a participating hospital, a participating skilled nursing facility, or participating home health agency, the institution will submit your claim for HI payment. This claim is handled by an "intermediary," an organization (usually an insurance company) within your state with which Medicare contracts to handle HI claims.

The intermediary decides whether the services submitted by the institution as part of your claim are covered under Medicare. You will receive a notice indicating why payment was denied for any services the intermediary determined could not be reimbursed. The institution that treated you will be reimbursed directly through the intermediary and charge you for the portion of the bill that was not paid by your HI.

REIMBURSEMENT UNDER SMI

The cost of service to you and amount of paperwork you have depends upon whether your doctor or medical equipment supplier accepts "assignment." If so, your doctor or supplier has agreed to accept what Medicare calls "approved charges" as payment in full and also to accept directly from Medicare the portion of "approved charges" that SMI pays (80 percent). If not, you may want to try to convince him or her otherwise, or even consider shopping around for a new doctor or supplier.

Doctors and suppliers who allow you to "assign" your Medicare payments directly to them guarantee that you will not be responsible for paying any more for covered services than the portion of "reasonable charges" that your SMI does not cover (20 percent plus the $75 deductible, if applicable at the time of billing). They also do the paperwork, best handled by an office familiar with reimbursement procedures.

Your doctor or supplier who accepts assignment will submit bills for health care services covered under your SMI protection directly to the organization—the "Medicare carrier"—in your state that handles SMI claims. Your doctor or supplier will bill you for the portion of "approved charges" for covered services that Medicare does not pay plus all noncovered services. All Social Security offices and area agencies on aging have copies of the directory that lists the physicians and suppliers in your state who have agreed to accept assignment for a 12-month period. Your Medicare carrier has these directories for sale. In 1987, about 30 percent of physicians are "participating."

Non-participating doctors can choose to accept assignment for some patients or treatments and not for others. If assignment is not accepted, *and* if the doctor does not file the claim for you, then you will be billed directly. In turn, you should submit these bills to your medical carrier along with a completed "Patient's Request for Medicare Payment" form (1490-S). Call your Social Security office to get these forms and the address of your SMI carrier.

When you submit bills, be sure to fill out all the information and to enclose *itemized bills* with the following information:

- description of all services and supplies you received along with the charge, date, and place for each service or supply;
- the doctor or supplier of each service or supply;
- your name and Medicare health insurance number as they are printed on your Medicare cards;

You can include more than one bill from a number of doctors or suppliers with each "Request for Medicare Payment" form. It's a good idea to write "Medicare" on the outside of the envelope and to keep a copy of everything.

The carrier will then determine which services are covered and what constitutes approved charges. Payment for the portion of approved charges for which SMI is responsible will be made directly to you. The carrier will notify you about decisions to deny a claim and its reason for doing so.

Are there time limits for submission of SMI claims? Yes. You should always submit them no later than 15 months after the service was rendered, but sooner is obviously better. Can claims be made for outstanding bills of a deceased relative who was covered under Medicare? Yes. Contact your Social Security office to get information about this.

APPEALING A REIMBURSEMENT DECISION

Appeals procedures for HI claims and SMI claims are different, and there are two different HI appeals processes. If you question all or part of a decision on a HI claim, you should first call your Social Security office or Medicare intermediary and ask for an explanation. If you decide to appeal, call again and ask them to send the appropriate form, to give you advice on filling it out, and to whom you send it. Include your name, Medical Insurance number, date and place of treatment, the reason for the appeal (along with any supporting evidence you wish to include), and the name of the organization that denied the claim. Also, you should know that as a result of a recent change in the laws, a provider may represent beneficiaries on appeals and all claims (including technical denials) are appealable.

To appeal pre-admission decisions on surgery and decisions on length of hospital stays, ask for a PRO review. If you are not satisfied with the review and if you are appealing $200 or more in claims, you may request a hearing before an administrative law judge. If the amount is at least $2000, you may request review by the Appeals Council and, ultimately, by the federal district court. In general, you should act within 60 days of receiving notice of decisions at each level.

For other HI benefits, the appeals process begins with a request for a reconsideration through the Medicare intermediary, which can be sent either to the intermediary or your local Social Security office.

If you are appealing $100 or more in claims, you may request a hearing before an administrative law judge if your reconsideration is denied. You must act within 60 days of your notification about the reconsideration decision. If you disagree with the decision of the ALJ and the amount in question is at least $1000, you may request, within 60 days, a review by the Appeals Council of the Office of Hearings and Appeals. The final level of appeal is in the federal district court.

To appeal all or part of a decision on a SMI claim, within six months of being notified about the initial decision, request the carrier to reconsider your initial claim. Send a written request to your carrier or local Social Security office and include the same information you would for an HI claim. If you still disagree with the decision and if the dispute involves $100 or more, you may request a hearing by the carrier within six months of the notice of the decision on your first appeal. If you still disagree with the decision and the amount in question is

$500 or more, a recent change in the law now allows you to appeal to the ALJ level. After that, you may appeal to the federal district if the amount in question is over $1000.

IMPORTANT MEDICARE PUBLICATIONS

For more information about Medicare benefits and Medicare in general, call your Social Security office and ask them to send copies of *Your Medicare Handbook* and *A Brief Explanation of Medicare*. If your efforts to find out something about Medicare come to no avail, you may want to pay for a long distance call to the national headquarters of the Health Care Financing Administration in Baltimore, Maryland (1-301-594-8715). But first consider calling your Congressman or Congresswoman.

RECENT CHANGES AND CURRENT DEBATE

Recent legislative and administrative changes in the Medicare program have been mainly of two types: (1) changes in provider reimbursements, especially for hospitals, which have produced much of the savings in Medicare, and (2) increases in premiums, deductibles, and copayments that increase out-of-pocket costs to beneficiaries. More recently, the focus of policy discussions has shifted to include concerns for quality of care.

Recent Changes in Provider Reimbursements. The trend in changes has been toward placing more limits on allowable costs for reimbursement purposes and cost controls on the providers of services to Medicare beneficiaries, especially hospitals.

The 1983 amendments to the Social Security Act provided for the phase-in of an entirely new way of reimbursing hospitals. In the past, they were reimbursed by Medicare after rendering the service. Under the new mechanism, which will be fully phased in by the end of 1988, hospitals will be reimbursed before they supply a Medicare-covered service. The amount of

Medicare reimbursement hospitals receive depends on a patient's diagnosis. Hospital admissions are generally classified into diagnosis-related groups (DRGs) and the hospital is paid an amount for each patient according to his or her DRG. Hospitals must absorb losses if a patient's care costs more than the DRG reimbursement; they are rewarded with "profits" if their costs are less than the DRG's set rate.

This approach provides hospitals with a strong incentive to hold down costs and is helping to slow the increase in health costs. Concerns have been expressed, however, about possible drawbacks. For instance, a 1985 field investigation conducted by the U.S. Senate Committee on Aging found evidence of:

- inappropriate or premature hospital discharge of some seriously ill Medicare patients;
- many seriously ill patients and their families being given inadequate information about their options for post-hospital care and about their right to appeal discharge decisions;
- the denial of hospital admissions to some patients with complex cases as a way of avoiding taking "unprofitable" cases.

The growing awareness of the effect of the prospective payment system on quality of care has resulted in changes requiring hospitals to better inform Medicare patients about their rights, expanding the role of PROs to involve quality of care, and encouraging better discharge planning.

Since the prospective payment system was begun, some have felt that a significant portion of savings generated by this reimbursement change would involve little more than cost shifting. To make up for the reduction in Medicare revenues, hospitals might increase charges to private (non-Medicare) patients, shifting some of the cost onto private insurers, consumers of health care, and employers who pay insurance premiums. Restricting cost-containment measures primarily to Medicare could ultimately lead to even more of a two-class medical system than currently exists, composed of hospitals and service providers who will treat only private patients and those who treat primarily Medicare and other publicly financed patients. As an alternative, some suggest cost containment measures should be implemented across the entire health care system.

Effects of Recent Changes and Proposals on Out-of-Pocket Costs. Rising health care costs, the anticipated depletion of the HI Trust Fund in the late-1990s and large federal deficits have led to serious consideration of proposals requiring greater cost sharing by beneficiaries and their families.

Some have been implemented. The Medicare HI deduction was increased from $304 in 1982 to $520 in 1987 creating, as the American Association of Retired Persons notes, financial barriers to health care access for some elderly and disabled persons. Daily hospital insurance copayments have also increased, as have SMI monthly premiums.

In short, a significant portion of recent savings in Medicare expenditures result directly from shifting a larger portion of the cost of care onto beneficiaries and their families. And, there remain many critical services, especially those related to mental illness and long term care, for which Medicare provides only minimal, if any, payment at all.

There may be more to come. For instance, the Reagan administration has proposed substantial increases in the HI copayments, and in 1986, proposed raising the SMI premium to 35 percent of program costs, delaying the age of Medicare eligibility by about one month, increasing the SMI deductible, and requiring copayments for home health services where none now exist.

Similarly, the administration-appointed 1983 Advisory Council on Social Security recommended increasing the eligibility age for full benefits from 65 to 67, over a 12-year period beginning in 1990. This would reduce Medicare costs, primarily at the expense of the sickest persons among those aged 65 and 66, for it is the very sick and the dying who account for the bulk of Medicare expenditures. The argument that because people are living longer it's all right to raise the age of eligibility for Medicare just doesn't hold water. Very sick and dying people aged 65 and 66 in the year 2002 will be no less sick or less likely to die than similarly aged persons who are very sick and dying in 1987.

In general, the administration's health care proposals are built on the premise that cost sharing will greatly discourage demand for health care services, reduce Medicare costs, and create competitive incentives to contain spiraling medical costs. No one doubts that these proposals would reduce Medicare costs, but their effect on quality of care and the fairness of these proposals is in dispute.

During the next few years many Medicare financing proposals will be debated and some people will predict the imminent collapse of the program. Medicare's financing problems are real and complex, but Congress can no more allow Medicare to "collapse" than it could allow the Social Security cash programs to do so.

In fact, this and other problems in the health care system could combine to encourage reforms which would strengthen the entire health care system. To do so, however, will require the development of policies that maintain a balance between several cherished goals, including quality of care, access to care, efficiency and cost-containment, and affordable care.

OTHER PUBLIC PROGRAMS

Although this book is about Social Security and Medicare benefits, there are some other public benefits about which you should know.

SSI FOR AGED, BLIND AND DISABLED PERSONS

The 1972 amendments of the Social Security Act created the Supplemental Security Income (SSI) program. Beginning in 1974, SSI replaced existing state public assistance programs of Old-Age Assistance, Aid to the Blind, and Aid to the Permanently and Totally Disabled.

SSI Benefits. SSI provides monthly cash payments to about 4.2 million aged and disabled and blind persons, a total in federal and state expenditure of about $12.3 billion in 1987. Through SSI, the federal government guarantees low income aged and the blind and disabled of all ages a minimum income—$510 for a couple and $340 for single persons in 1987—to those who meet eligibility criteria. Some states also provide a substantial supplement to the federal SSI payment.

Although administered by the Social Security Administration, receipt of a benefit does not require previous payroll tax contributions. Your local Social Security office handles virtually all SSI applications. (Some people who live in states that administer their own supplements should apply for the state supplement to the federal SSI guarantee at the state public assistance [public welfare] office).

Like Social Security cash benefits, SSI benefits are protected against inflation by automatic cost-of-living adjustments.

Automatic adjustments are made in the December check (payable in January) whenever the yearly increase in inflation is 0.1 percent or more (after rounding).

Can persons who receive Social Security cash benefits also qualify for SSI? Yes. For instance, if you received a monthly Social Security check in 1987 of less than $360 as an individual, or of less than $530 as a couple, you may be eligible to receive a SSI check, too. In states that provide SSI supplements, you may be eligible for the state supplement even if your Social Security cash benefits are above those amounts.

Can people who work receive SSI benefits? Yes. Currently the first $65 of earned income in any month does not affect your SSI benefits. After that, SSI benefits are reduced by one dollar for every two dollars of earnings.

Living arrangements can affect benefit levels. Benefits can be reduced by up to one-third for SSI beneficiaries who live in someone else's household. Beneficiaries receiving institutional care funded by Medicaid can receive up to $25 in SSI benefits. People in public non-Medicaid funded institutions (i.e., state-funded mental hospitals) are not eligible for SSI benefits.

SSI beneficiaries are usually eligible for Medicaid benefits that cover most of their health care costs. SSI recipients usually are eligible automatically for Food Stamps, except in California and Wisconsin, which add in the value of food stamps in order to increase the value of their state SSI supplemental payment. And SSI beneficiaries may also be eligible for social services (e.g., transportation or homemaker service) provided through their state or local department of public assistance (public welfare). For information about these services, contact your local Social Security office or public assistance office, sometimes called the Department of Social Services.

Eligibility. SSI provides benefits to low-income people with limited resources aged 65 and over and the blind and disabled of any age. The criteria and application process for SSI disability benefits are essentially the same as that for Social Security disability benefits (see Chapter 10), except that SSI has both an income and an assets test.

Can SSI administrative decisions be appealed? Yes, many can. Appeals must be made within 60 days of when you are notified of a decision. You must appeal in 10 days if you are appealing a decision to reduce or terminate SSI disability benefits and if you want your checks to continue as they were during the first stage of your appeal.

If you think you or a friend may be eligible, call your local Social Security Administration office. Many people are entitled to SSI, but fail to apply. Remember, if you qualify for SSI you will generally also be eligible for Medicaid and Food Stamps.

MEDICAID BENEFITS

Medicaid provides access to needed health services for 23.6 million low-income Americans: about 11.4 million children under 21; 3.3 million age 65 and over; 3 million disabled; and 5.8 million other adults. Medicaid costs, about $37.6 billion in 1987, are shared by both the federal and state governments. Over two-thirds of Medicaid expenditures are for aged and disabled beneficiaries.

Unlike Medicare, Medicaid is means tested. It is not funded from payroll taxes but draws instead from federal, state, and local general tax revenues. Also, unlike Medicare, Medicaid also spends a substantial portion of its funds on long-term care. About 40 percent of Medicaid expenditures go for long-term care of the elderly in nursing homes. Another large chunk of its budget funds much of the institutional care of the mentally retarded. In fact, one of Medicaid's drawbacks is that relatively little is spent on home health care, prevention, or primary care.

Benefits. Benefits vary by state. To be eligible for federal matching funds, all states must, at a minimum, offer the following minimum services to people defined as "categorically needy" (usually persons receiving SSI or AFDC): inpatient hospital services, outpatient hospital services, laboratory and X-ray services, skilled nursing facility for those over age 21 (SNF), home health services for those eligible for SNF care, regular health screening, diagnosis and treatment for those under 21, family planning services and supplies, and physician services.

Eligibility. Eligibility requires that a person be defined as either "categorically needy" or "medically needy." All states include AFDC and SSI beneficiaries as the categorically needy, although some require SSI recipients to meet stricter eligibility criteria than were in effect in 1972. Some states also include, as the categorically needy, people who receive SSI supplements, those who would be eligible for cash benefits except that they reside in institutions, financially eligible children under 21, unemployed fathers and their families or children under 21, and pregnant women before the sixth month of pregnancy.

States may also elect to cover "medically needy" persons: aged; blind; disabled; or members of families with dependent children whose incomes—after deducting medical expenses—fall below the state standard of need.

Local departments of public assistance (public welfare) generally take Medicaid applications. Hospitals and other service-providing organizations sometimes assist persons in applying. Eligibility requires meeting both income and assets tests. A recent change in the law gives states the option of applying a more liberal income test to infants under age one, to pregnant women, eventually to children ages one through 4, and *if* states choose these liberalizations, also to the elderly and disabled.

Medicaid Issues. Reductions in federal Medicaid revenues, concerns over the cost of the program to states, and rising medical costs have contributed to a general tightening of eligibility and benefits in many states. Federal legislation passed in 1981 and 1982, with strong support of the Reagan administration, reduced the amount of federal funding going to states and allowed states for the first time to:

- require the children of nursing home residents to pay some of the costs of their parents' care, a provision that could greatly increase the financial responsibilities of many middle-aged

people and that could also be very unsettling for disabled aged people who do not wish to be a burden on their families;
- place a lien on the property of institutionalized Medicaid beneficiaries if this property is not needed by the recipient, spouse, sibling, disabled or dependent children;
- require copayments of two dollars or less for certain Medicaid services—a provision that might discourage some low-income persons from receiving treatment until health problems are so bad as to require more expensive interventions.

Long-term care remains an important Medicaid issue. Also, the tightening of reimbursements and the growing restrictions on Medicaid benefits are making it more difficult for beneficiaries to receive the same level of care as non-recipients. The proportion of health care providers willing to accept Medicaid beneficiaries is shrinking. Another issue concerns the many people of all ages who need health care protection, but are ineligible for Medicaid or any other public or private health care program.

This is becoming an increasingly important problem. Witness: between 1975 and 1983, as a result of changes in eligibility in Aid to Families with Dependent Children and Medicaid, the proportion of low-income persons protected by Medicaid fell from 63 to 46 percent.

FOOD STAMPS

Eligibility has been tightened somewhat and the value of food stamps reduced slightly during the past few years, but the Food Stamp program remains a major income supplement for more than 21 million Americans who meet its income and assets tests. In general, the maximum monthly value of food stamps through September of 1987 is $81 for a single person, $149 for a couple and $271 for a family of four. (Maximum benefit levels are higher in Alaska, Hawaii, Guam, and the Virgin Islands, and lower in Puerto Rico.)

The program is federally funded and administered by the states. To find out more about it, contact your state or local Department of Public Assistance or public welfare, or your Social Security Administration office.

VETERAN'S BENEFITS

If you're a veteran discharged under other than dishonorable conditions or a surviving dependent of such a veteran, you or members of your family might be eligible for veteran's cash or medical benefits. Call the Veteran's Administration (VA). Their number is listed in the telephone directory under U.S. Government, Veterans Administration or Veterans Benefits, Information and Assistance, or each state has a toll free "800" number for veteran's information which you can get by calling the "800" information operator (1-800-555-1212). Have your Social Security number and Military Service Number handy.

Veteran's Compensation benefits are paid to those whose disability or illness occurred or was aggravated during active duty. Payments are based on the degree of disability. There are no means tests and, under certain circumstances, spouses and dependent children can receive benefits.

Veteran's Pensions are paid to veterans of the Mexican border period, World War I, World War II, the Korean War and the Vietnam War who meet certain income limitations. To qualify, a veteran must also be 65 or over and not working, or have a nonservice-connected, permanent, and total disability. The presence of a spouse and/or dependent children, or both, or the need for regular assistance may increase the size of the pension. Survivors' pensions may also be available to widows or widowers, dependent children, or dependent adult children disabled before age 18.

Veteran's medical benefits include inpatient hospital treatment, outpatient treatment, home health services, nursing home care, alcohol and drug dependence treatment, and domiciliary care. Under certain circumstances, the spouses and dependent children of veterans are also eligible for medical benefits.

Other VA benefits include housing, employment training, burial services, vocational rehabilitation, and loans.

OTHER PUBLIC DISABILITY PROGRAMS

Worker's Compensation provides protection against loss of income, medical expenses, or death due to work-related injuries or death. With the exception of the Federal Employee Compensation program these are state-run and state-administered programs. If you have a work-related disability, temporary or permanent, or if you are the surviving spouse or dependent surviving child of a worker whose on-the-job injury resulted in death, you may be eligible to receive these benefits.

The Black Lung Program was established by the Federal Coal Mine Health and Safety Act of 1969 to provide benefits for miners totally disabled by black lung disease as well as spouses and certain dependents and certain survivors of such miners. Your local Social Security office accepts applications for these benefits.

The Railroad Retirement Program provides disability and retirement benefits to railroad industry employees as well as dependents' and survivors' benefits. The Railroad Retirement Board administers the program and has offices in major cities.

State and federal public employee pensions, the largest of which is the Federal Civil Service Retirement System, also provide disability and retirement benefits and survivors' benefits.

UNEMPLOYMENT COMPENSATION

State Unemployment Compensation programs, often called Unemployment Insurance, provide partial wage replacement over a limited period of time for recently employed persons who are now unemployed. Contact your state's unemployment office for information.

OTHER PUBLIC ASSISTANCE BENEFITS

Aid to Families with Dependent Children (AFDC) provides cash benefits to low-income dependent children—and their adult caretakers—who have been deprived of parental care or support because of the absence, incapacity, death, or unemployment of their fathers or mothers.

General assistance programs are funded by many state and local governments. These are often programs of last resort for low-income adults without dependent children who do not qualify for SSI or any other federally-funded programs. In addition to being means tested, eligibility often requires that applicants have work-limiting disabilities.

Programs also exist to assist with payment of fuel bills, to help during emergencies, and to assist refugees under certain circumstances. State or local public assistance (public welfare) offices can provide information about these programs, AFDC, and general assistance.

HOUSING PROGRAMS

A variety of publicly supported housing programs are available to low-income families, the disabled, the aged, and to moderate-income aged persons, too. Local housing authorities, city halls, and multi-purpose senior citizen centers can generally provide information about these programs; nonprofit organizations, such as churches, synagogues, and social agencies involved with the construction of nonprofit housing for the elderly, can often supply information as well.

SOCIAL SERVICES

Public social services are administered primarily through state and local departments of public assistance (Departments of Social Services and Public Welfare). These services (some of which are available to low-income persons, others to everyone) include homemaker, chore and health services, transportation, home-delivered meals, adult day centers, legal services, protective services, information and referral, and many services for children. SSI beneficiaries and other low-income aged and disabled persons are very likely to be eligible.

Multi-purpose Senior Citizens Centers provide access to a large range of programs and services for people aged 60 and over. These centers provide such services as meals through the Older Americans Act Nutrition program, legal services, volunteer opportunities, courses, employment referral, information and referral, and health screening. Other agencies serving older constituencies frequently take applications and offer services through multi-purpose senior centers.

Vocational rehabilitation services are designed to assist disabled people to become employable and live independently. Services provided through state vocational rehab agencies include employment training, specialized equipment and prostheses, counseling and educational opportunities.

Private social service agencies offer a full range of social services to people of all ages under both religious and nonreligious auspices. Special services are often available for the elderly. These agencies can be found throughout the country.

Community mental health centers also provide services to people of all ages.

THE FUTURE OF SOCIAL SECURITY AND MEDICARE

Social Security is over 50 years old and the 25th anniversary of Medicare is only a few years away. Together, these programs have enhanced and become part of our way of life—critical institutions supporting our democratic society. But, what of the future?

While much progress has been made toward the goal of economic security for all Americans, much remains to be done. And, as in the past, it is reasonable to expect that significant policy questions will arise from time to time. Here are a few that may be important during the next 20 years.

CONFIDENCE IN SOCIAL SECURITY

On signing the 1983 Amendments to the Social Security Act into law, President Reagan said, "It assures our elderly that America will always keep promises made in troubled times a half-century ago. It assures those who are still working that they, too, have a pact with the future." Since then, as you know, Social Security has actually run larger yearly surpluses than were projected. It remains a viable and sound program. Further, there is much public support across all age groups for the program with, for example, a National Survey by Yankelovich, Skelley and White in 1985 indicating that among Americans age 25 and over 98% believe Social Security is an essential source of income for many elderly and 88% want it to continue.

Yet, in spite of the widespread public support for Social Security and its strong financial position, the public—especially the young—lack confidence in the program.

One reason is that most younger Americans grew up taking Social Security for granted without really understanding the concept of social insurance, its roots in an era of economic insecurity, or what America would be like without it.

Also, the concept of Social Security has often been misunderstood. First, there was the mistaken belief that payroll tax contributions go into some sort of account with your name on it, only to be drawn at retirement, disability, or death. Then came the myth that Social Security could go broke. Proclamations that the "sky is falling" whenever problems arise have affected the public's confidence in Social Security.

And, over the past 20 years we have seen a general decline in public faith in institutions generally, including the government. So it should come as no surprise that confidence has also declined in a program whose very integrity is based on the government's promise to maintain its commitments.

Facing problems squarely, as the 1983 amendments did, is a good step in improving public confidence. And, as the funds accumulate as a result of these amendments, confidence in Social Security will increase. We must understand the fact that as the economy and society change, adjustments will be needed in Social Security, but this need for adjustments does not mean the program is in deep trouble. In fact, the ability to adapt to changing circumstances is one of its greatest strengths.

FINANCING MEDICARE

Medicare is facing a financing problem, but it extends well beyond Medicare itself. To a large extent, the problem is a result of a health care system that lacks system-wide cost controls. The solution, therefore, requires more fundamental changes than simply increasing Medicare revenues or decreasing program expenditures. Ultimately, we probably need to move toward a better, planned health care system with regulations designed to restrain costs while also ensuring quality of care.

But even if effective cost containment mechanisms were in

place now, costs for public medical care of the aged and disabled would still be high and would be projected to be higher yet as more people live to the later old ages (75 and over), a period in life during which medical costs are quite high. Even so, as a society, we are not likely to turn back from providing access through Medicare to health care for the disabled and the elderly, in part because failure to provide such care is also expensive—particularly to individuals and their families who would otherwise be faced with large and often unexpected health care bills for the aged and their families.

What should we do? In addition to instituting cost-containment measures, one way or another, we will need to increase tax revenues. Several options should be given serious consideration, including: raising cigarette and alcohol taxes with the proceeds earmarked for Medicare; modest income-tax surcharge earmarked for Medicare; counting a portion of the value of Medicare coverage as taxable income so that higher-income aged and disabled beneficiaries would pay additional taxes earmarked to the Medicare trust funds; increased payroll taxation for the HI Trust Fund; greater use of general revenues to fund Medicare beginning in the mid to late 1990s.

No matter what combination of means is used to resolve Medicare's financing problems, three goals should be paramount: the need to protect all individuals and their family members of all ages from the high cost of hospitalization; access to quality health care; and the equitable distribution of the cost of financing Medicare among *all* groups.

MEDICARE VOUCHERS

What about the proposal put forth by the Reagan administration to give Medicare beneficiaries a choice between receiving Medicare protection or a voucher that they could use to purchase private insurance? They could keep the difference between the selected plan cost and the voucher's value. Supporters claim the proposal would cut Medicare costs and contain health care costs by introducing greater competition. Consumers, it is believed, would become cost-conscious and select plans with more out-of-pocket expenses, thereby making them more sensitive to the cost of medical care.

But there are massive problems with the voucher proposals. The younger and healthier elderly and disabled might select cheaper plans with limited benefits, only to find several years later that their health is such that they then need more comprehensive coverage offered through other plans. Allowing beneficiaries to "opt out" would leave Medicare with an insurance pool composed disproportionately of the oldest and least healthy aged and disabled people. Costs per person would skyrocket and the political support of the program decline. Medicare vouchers ultimately would result in greatly increased welfare costs for medical care for some people or greatly decreased access and quality of care for many.

In short, vouchers aren't a terribly good idea if you want to protect against the cost of medical care and provide access to health care. They are simply a back-handed way to cap costs.

LONG-TERM CARE

Today, the single biggest threat to the economic well-being of the elderly and their families comes from the high costs of providing long-term care services, at home or in institutions, to the chronically ill elderly. While it is estimated that at any one point in time only 5 percent of the elderly are in nursing homes and 7 to 12 percent are receiving some assistance at home, research suggests the majority of persons who reach age 65 will need long-term care services at some point during their old age.

The great majority of the disabled elderly are cared for by family members. Even so, 1) the growth of the aged population (especially 85 and over), 2) generally smaller families, resulting in fewer relatives per disabled older person, and 3) the increased likelihood that working aged women—who traditionally have been the primary care givers—are in paid employment and, therefore, not able to provide as much home care, all mean that the need for community and institutionally-based long-term care services will expand.

Given this increasing need, we, as a society, must plan for increased federal expenditures and better coordination of long-term care services at both the community and institutional levels. Families can and do provide much care, but they also need assistance from supportive public policies.

CATASTROPHIC COSTS

As this book is going into print, there is much talk about adding protection under Medicare against certain catastrophic health care costs. The Reagan administration has proposed capping out-of-pocket expenses for hospital and certain other services provided under Medicare at $2000 a year. Beneficiaries would pay an additional $4.92 a month under the Medicare SMI program to receive this protection.

The proposal does not, however, cover long-term care—the source of most catastrophic costs for the elderly and disabled. Consequently, as Republican Senator John Heinz has stated, "five of six older Americans with catastrophic costs will not be helped." Even so, it is encouraging that catastrophic costs are being seriously discussed. Hopefully, this may be the first step in providing fully adequate protection against the risk of catastrophic long-term care costs Americans of all ages and in assuring that all—especially the 37 million who are without health protection of any kind—have health care coverage.

PREVENTIVE CARE AND RESEARCH

Preventive services such as periodic physicals, most drugs, much health screening, dentures, eyeglasses, and hearing aids are not covered under Medicare. Because the failure to cover preventative services can lead to hospitalizations which might have been avoided, there is a clear need to provide greater incentive for beneficiaries to seek preventive services.

Another type of preventive strategy should also be pursued by those concerned with quality of life and health care costs. Biomedical and social research can make a phenomenal difference in the lives of Americans. For example, research has recently shown that proper diet and exercise—especially adequate calcium intake for women in middle age and old age—can greatly reduce the risk of osteoporosis. Research that might lead to ways of delaying the onset (or perhaps someday eliminating) certain chronic diseases (e.g. Alzheimer's) could change the face of old age for future generations of retirees.

WOMEN AND SOCIAL SECURITY

In contrast to the time in which Social Security was enacted, today about one-half of all married women are in paid jobs, and roughly two out of five new marriages are expected to end in divorce. Most people's attitudes about the roles of men and women have changed. Marriages are seen as partnerships of equals. Yet, Social Security has not fully adjusted to these changes.

The 1981 National Commission on Social Security pointed out that "it would be unfair to say that Social Security throughout its history has not reflected a concern for providing adequate protection for women." It cited enactment of wives' and widows' benefits in 1940, the way the benefit formula provides proportionally larger benefits to low-wage workers, who are often women, and other aspects of the law as evidence. What are now called spouse and widow's or widower's benefits help maintain the standard of living of many older women.

Still, there remain some problems that many consider of particular concern to women: the high proportion of widows with poverty level incomes; the lack of disability protection for homemakers; the inadequacy of benefits for divorced spouses; lack of recognition of the economic worth of work performed in the home, such as child-rearing; and that benefits paid to a retired couple in which only one spouse was employed are usually higher than benefits paid to couples with similar total earnings in which both spouses were employed.

Earnings sharing is a partial solution favored by some. The earnings-sharing concept is extremely attractive because it recognizes that marriage, besides being an emotional partnership, is also an economic partnership, with each partner having a right to an equal share of the fruits of their joint effort. Unlike current law, earnings sharing would allow a husband and wife, or divorced spouses, each, to be credited with one-half of the total earnings of the couple during marriage. Retirement or disability benefits would then be based on one-half of the combined earnings during marriage plus any earnings from work performed before or after the marriage.

But, earnings sharing also has major limitations. To move to a full earnings-sharing proposal without increasing the overall cost of Social Security would require substantial reductions in benefits for some. Such a solution that sacrifices the interests of one group for another (e.g. homemakers for working wives) is not desirable.

Fair resolution of the problems of special concern to women will require additional revenues. Some modified earnings-sharings proposals could be incorporated into the law. But, more will be needed to alleviate the very severe economic problems faced by some of the current generation of older women.

THE SOCIAL SECURITY SURPLUS

In contrast to a few years ago when national attention was riveted to the anticipated shortfalls in the OASDI trust funds, Social Security now faces a relatively delightful problem—what to do about large surpluses. Since the enactment of the 1983 amendments, the combined OASDI trust fund has actually experienced yearly surpluses. And shortly after 1988 and 1990 payroll tax increases go into effect, very large surpluses are anticipated. In fact, it is likely that from 2005 through 2025 the combined trust fund during each year will have a large earnings reserve, four or five times as much money as needed to make payments in the course of these years. It's anticipated that this surplus will be drawn down primarily from 2025 through 2050.

The surpluses raise numerous questions, including their potential effect on savings and the economy, how these funds should be invested, and whether changes should be made at some point in the future to prevent such large surpluses from occurring. For now, however, it's good to know that more money is going into the combined trust fund than coming out.

SHOULD ELIGIBILITY AGE BE RAISED?

Undoubtedly the question of whether raising the eligibility age for full benefits is desirable policy will be reviewed before the gradual phasing-in of new ages begins in 2000. If the normal retirement age is raised, it would be unconscionable without also substantially liberalizing the disability criteria as applied to older workers. In fact, this type of change would be good policy under the current age levels because among the many who retire early now and accept permanently reduced benefits, a significant proportion do so because their health makes employment in their occupation extremely difficult, although their health is not so bad that they meet the very strict DI standards.

IMPROVED SSI BENEFITS

The economic status of aged and disabled persons has improved greatly over the past 25 years. Even so, about 3.3 million people 65 and over (12.6 percent) have incomes below the official poverty threshold—$5156 for an aged individual and $6503 for an aged couple in 1985.

What can be done? The simplest and most efficient thing to do is increase the federal SSI benefit to the poverty line. Providing a minimum income equal to the poverty line for aged and disabled citizens is both a modest and attainable goal.

And, it's also time to concentrate on providing sufficient jobs paying above poverty wages and improving unemployment insurance and public assistance programs so that none of our citizens need to be poor—especially the 21 percent of the nation's children (about 13 million) who are now poor. Not only is this poverty unnecessary and unjust, but as a report recently issued by the Gerontological Society of America notes, as we prepare for the retirement of the baby boomers we simply must assure that the generation that will support them in their retirement years will be well-educated and productive.

THE FUTURE OF SOCIAL SECURITY

President Roosevelt and other framers of the Social Security Act had a vision of a social insurance program that would eventually grow to protect against major risks experienced by everyone. As we have seen, protection has expanded to include substantial retirement, survivors', and disability benefits, as well as health insurance benefits for the aged and disabled.

Will new forms of protection be added? No one really knows. If the economy expands, at even modest rates, we as a nation will be able to afford more Social Security as time goes on.

Over the long run we probably will choose to add some programs like long-term care insurance, national health insurance, or to extend Medicare protection to new groups. With sufficient resources, we may choose to develop entirely new programs, like infant care insurance, designed to underwrite family life by alleviating some of the financial stress experienced by many young families during the early years of child-rearing and also to make it more possible for a parent to stay home if desired, through the provision of cash benefits and health coverage for families with children under one year old.

No one knows what the future will bring. But that Social Security has consistently proved itself able to respond to changing social conditions and unexpected economic events is one of its great strengths and should be a source of confidence in the essential American institution. To quote Wilbur J. Cohen, who has been involved with virtually every major Social Security decision since 1934, when he worked on the committee that helped plan the program: "I do not know what the shape or form of Social Security will be on its one hundredth anniversary in the year 2035, but I will predict that Social Security will still be an important institution responding to the needs of the society and the economy of that time."

INDEX

Administrative law judges (ALG), 40, 41, 78, 96
Aid to Families with Dependent Children (AFDC), 80, 108
Appeals
 disability decisions, 77
 eligibility decisions, 46-47
 reimbursement decisions, 95-96
 SSI decisions, 103
Average Indexed Monthly Earnings (AIME), 52-56, 62, 73, 74

Ball, Robert M., 13
Benefits
 applying for, 44-49, 83-85
 direct deposit, 48
 retirement, 11, 50-57, 58-65
 taxing, 32-33
 unemployment, 13, 107
Black Lung Program, 107
Blindness, 51, 75, 101-103, 104

Catastrophic costs, 114
Children's benefits, 60, 61-62
Civil Service Retirement System (CSRS), 35
Cohen, Wilbur, 12, 118
Cost-of-living adjustments (COLA), 29, 30-31, 65

Death in family, 45
Death payment, 70
Deductible, 87, 97
Delayed Retirement Benefit, 58-59
Dependent children's and grandchildren's benefits, 61
Diagnosis-related group (DRGs), 98
Disability Benefits Reform Act of 1984, 41-42
Disability determination service (DDS), 75
Disability Insurance (DI), 13, 18, 19, 29, 32
Disability Insurance Trust Fund, 18-21, 34, 116
Disabled child's benefit, 60, 62
Disabled widow(er)s, 67-68, 79
Disabled workers, 25, 46, 51, 57, 62, 71-72, 84
 benefits, 38-42, 71-79, 101-103
 criterion, 74-75

Divorced spouses, 60-61
Doctor's services, 90, 94-95

Early Retirement Benefit, 58
Earnings, 7, 9, 16-17, 18-20, 50-51
 benefit under two, 63-64
 sharing, 115-116
 test, 64-65, 67
Eligibility
 age of, 29, 36-38, 51, 117
 appealing decision, 46-47
 disability, 74-75
Medicaid, 104
Medicare, 82-83
SSI, 102

Family benefits, 59-62, 66-70, 72, 103, 108
Family maximum, 62, 67, 74
Federal Employers Retirement System (FERS), 35
Financing problems, 18-22, 26-29, 100, 111-112
Food Stamps, 42, 102, 105

Government Pension offset, 62-63
Grandchildren benefits, 61

Heinz III, Senator John, 39, 114
Home health care benefits, 88, 92
Hospice care for dying persons, 88-89
Hospital care, 86-87
Hospital Insurance (HI), 13, 15, 81, 82, 83, 86-89, 93-94
Hospital Insurance Trust Fund, 18, 34, 35

Inpatient care, 86-88
Insurance, private, 13-16

Kidney failure, 45, 82, 85, 92

Long-term care, 113
Lump sum death payment, 70

Medicaid, 13, 25, 81, 102
 benefits, 103
 eligibility, 104
 issues, 104-105
 vs. Medicare, 80
Medical bills, HI payment, 93-94

Medicare, 13, 16, 18-22, 23, 25-26, 80-100
  benefits, 78, 80-100
  changes, recent, 97-100
  co-payments, 87
  eligibility, 82-83
  enrolling, 83-86
  financing, 18-22, 100, 111-112
  vouchers, 112-113
  "Medigap" policy, 85

National Commission on Social Security Reform, 28-29
Nonprofit organization employees, 36
Nursing facility, 88

Old-Age and Survivors Insurance (OASI), 13, 18, 19
Old-Age Survivors' Insurance Trust Fund, 18-21, 29, 32, 34, 116
Outpatient hospital services, 90-91

Parent's benefits, 70
Payroll tax, 14, 18
  1983 Amendments, 34-35
Peer Review Organizations (PROs), 92-93, 98
Pepper, Claude, 28, 38
Preventitive care and research, 114
Primary Insurance Amount (PIA), 51-57, 62, 66-68, 74
Psychiatric care, 87-88

Railroad Retirement Program, 32, 82-83, 107
Reagan, President Ronald, 27-28, 29
Reimbursement under SMI, 94-96
Remarriage, 68-69
Representative payee, 46
Retirement
  age, 36-38, 59-60, 117
  benefits, 11, 58-65
Review process, disability, 38-40, 41, 77-78
Roosevelt, President Franklin, 24-25, 118

Roybal, Edward R., 6, 43

Self-employed, 34-35
Social Security
  applying for benefits, 44-49
  benefit amounts, determining, 50-57
  cards, 42, 44-45
  checks, 42
  disability, 71-79
  financing problems, 18-22, 26-29
  future issues, 110-118
  history of, 23-29
  retirement benefits, 58-65
  survivor's benefits, 66-70
  value of, 7-12
Social Security Act, 13, 19, 25
  amendments, 19, 25-29, 30-37, 65, 73, 97, 101, 110
Spouse benefits, 59-60
State employee pensions, 107
Supplemental Medical Insurance (SMI), 13, 18, 20, 81, 84-86, 94-95
  reimbursement, 93-96
Supplementary Medical Insurance Trust Fund, 18
Supplemental Security Income (SSI), 17, 26, 38-42, 44, 71, 74, 78, 80, 82, 83, 101-103, 117-118
Survivor's benefits, 25, 66-70

Taxation of benefits, 32-33
Trial work period, 79
Unemployment compensation, 13, 107

Veteran's benefits, 106-107
Vocational rehabilitation, 76-77

Wage indexing amount, 51-56
Widows and widowers, 25, 37, 67-69, 84
Women and social security, 114-115
Workers, federal, 35
Workers' compensation, 107

Younger workers, 8-10, 37

Pharos Books are available at special discounts on bulk purchases for sales promotions, premiums, fundraising or educational use. For details, contact the Special Sales Department, Pharos Books, 200 Park Avenue, New York, NY 10166